Pinot

&

Pūhā

Nikki Perry & Kirsty Roby

1st edition, 2023

Edited by Evan Chan

ISBN 978-1-9911972-0-7 (paperback)

ISBN 978-1-9911972-5-2 (Kindle)

ISBN 978-1-9911972-1-4 (Epub)

Cover design and layout by Yummy Book Covers

Typeset in PT Serif, 10pt

To Jane Austen,
the queen of all romance writers,
and to Wellington on a good day.

Acknowledgements

Thank you so much for reading 'Pinot and Pūhā '

If you enjoy the book, please consider leaving a review.

If you would like to read more of our work, you can find information on our other books 'How to Marry Harry and 'The Missing Wife Life' here; www.nikkiperryandkirstyroby.com.

Thank you to Eva for the editing and to Yummy Book Covers for another beautiful cover design. Also to Dara for the book shop idea.

Pinot & Pūhā

Chapter one

"I should infinitely prefer a book."

Pride and Prejudice, Jane Austen

Melody Hawkins loved books. Not just reading, but the feel of a book in her hand. The anticipation of the first line on the first page. The woody, vanilla smell of the pages, the allure of the cover. The escape of a really good story. She also loved a good wine and a wedge of Brie. So the official opening night of her new shop 'PINOT AND PŪHĀ', a bookshop that also served wine and cheese platters, really was a dream come true.

It was going well. Local residents and business owners had turned up to check out the new store. The shelves were full of books. The wine flowed and the cheese platters looked perfect. Her best friend and business partner Ellie did the rounds, charming everyone with her usual easy chatter and grace.

But in truth, Mel was a little over smiling. Socialising did not come as easily for her and right now she'd rather be tucked up in her bed in the flat upstairs, reading an old favourite, in her pyjamas.

~

The brass bell over her door trilled again and she looked up from where she stood assembling a fruit platter at the little kitchen bench.

"Who the hell is that hottie?" Fern shrieked beside her, unsubtle as usual. Her sister always veered to the dramatic. She had arrived, typically, in a flurry of drama over her lack of a sitter, in a cloud of hairspray and cheap perfume, claiming she was dumping Chase, the latest man in her life. Trailing behind her had been Mel's nephews, Blade and Flint, who were now noticeably absent. Mel hoped they were with her mother.

The 'hottie' in question was a tall, blond, well-dressed man, with an easy smile and a bottle of Moët in one hand. Waving at Mel, he sauntered over, giving her a charmingly cheeky smile.

"This looks wonderful, congratulations, darling."

The 'darling' was new, Mel thought as she took the offered champagne from him.

"Thank you so much, but you didn't need to bring wine," she insisted.

"Well, it's not a celebration without the good stuff, is it?

And who might this be?" he asked, giving Fern a grin.

"Nate, this is my sister Fern. Fern, this is Nate Carmichael, my landlord."

Fern giggled up at him and held out a hand with long, pink manicured nails that Nate raised to his mouth and pressed a kiss against.

"Delighted to meet you, Fern." He gave her a wink. Fern giggled again. She was the only person Mel knew who actually giggled like she was twelve.

"The pleasure is all mine," she said in a breathy voice. "Where has Mel been hiding you then?"

Nate laughed before motioning to the assembled platter. "Can I help you with that, Mel?"

"No, no, that's fine, but can I get you a drink?"

"Well, why don't we crack open that bad boy?" Nate indicated the bubbles.

Mel wasn't overly keen on champagne right now if she was honest. She wasn't that eager to drink it after she'd been drinking red wine all night. It seemed rude not to have a glass with him though, so she went off in search of some flutes, promising to be back soon and suggesting to her sister that perhaps she should look for her boys. Fern waved her off, and Mel hoped she wouldn't say anything too embarrassing while she was gone.

After dropping the platter onto a coffee table and searching for appropriate glasses, Mel did a quick gather-up of empties and spotted her dad sneaking up the stairs to her little second-floor apartment, a book on World War Two planes tucked under his arm.

She found Nate in conversation with her mother and began heading their way, only to be waylaid by Colin Exeter. Colin was a local business owner with a small accountancy firm down the block. He was also somewhat pompous and a little unbearable.

"Melody, my dear." She tried not to grit her teeth. She wasn't keen on being called Melody and had told him that several times. And who under the age of eighty called people 'dear'? He was probably not even forty, she would say, but he was as dry and humourless as an old piece of toast, and much less appealing to have around.

"Have I told you how charming you look tonight?" he continued. "Quite the part, although I do believe some of your guests perhaps didn't follow the dress code?"

"Dress code? And please, Mel is fine."

Mel had on a black dress and pearls. She generally tended towards plain and classic as a look. Colin, she noted, wore a brown suit. It was polyester, and ill fitting. He had a red pinstripe tie and brown pleather shoes.

"Well, you would surely expect a certain level of respectability, for an evening literary event of this sort." Colin gestured with a shiny brown sleeve around the room. "It's a bit disappointing to see such a wanton disregard of social niceties is all I'm saying." He looked pointedly at her mother.

A headache had started at the base of her neck. Colin tended to have this effect on her. He had been hanging around since she and Ellie began work on the building back in July. His constant need to discuss social standing and general etiquette was enough to test the patience of a saint. Mel could feel her halo slipping.

"I did wonder actually, Melody," he said in his nasally voice, "if perhaps I might convince you to accompany me to dinner some night, where we could get to know each other better, away from our respective workplaces?"

"I'm so sorry, Colin, but I'm afraid I'm going to be working most nights, now that our liquor licence has come through." Mel tried to look slightly crestfallen. "But thank you."

Colin looked set to argue, so she quickly excused herself. Nate and her mother were still talking. Her mother looked in her element, gripping Nate's arm, head back, laughing a tinkling laugh with her long grey hair hanging down the back of her floral maxi dress.

"Melly, love, your landlord is a hoot," her mother declared when she saw Mel.

Nate gave her a smile and indicated the bottle. "Shall I do the honours?"

Passing him the champagne, Mel held out the flutes to be filled. "I see you've met my mother."

"I have and now I can see where you get your good looks from," he told her. Marion beamed.

It was a nice compliment. Marion was still a stunning woman, but Mel didn't look much like her mother at all.

She was very much like her father, in fact. She had both his height and olive colouring, along with his hazel eyes and dark hair. Fern was far more like their mother. Petite and pale with more delicate features and blue eyes.

"I was just telling Nate about my latest project," Marion told Mel. "These walls would be perfect for displaying artwork on."

Mel murmured in a noncommittal way, her smile slipping further. She loved her mother, she did, but Marion had recently decided she needed to unleash her creativity through the medium of oil paint, and was currently in an abstract expressionism phase. Her work was, quite frankly, to Mel's eye, horrendous. She was no expert of course, but she was ninety-eight per cent sure the rest of the world would agree with her assessment.

From the corner of her eye, she saw a flash of red and then there was her nephew, superhero cape waving behind him, and his older brother looking stricken, a few steps behind.

"Wait, no, Flinny," Blade called, and then Flint was upon them, a bundle of hyperactivity and loud shrieking. He gripped onto Nate's leg and attempted to climb the side of him, causing him to jerk and slosh champagne down Marion's dress in surprise.

"Fuck, sorry," Nate told her, before looking down at the small child and frowning.

"You said a bad word," Flint declared, lifting a hand and sucking on his finger. His very sticky finger, Mel observed.

"Flint. Get off Nate," she ordered, peeling him away from his pant leg. "What is that all over your hands?"

"I'm sorry, Aunty Mel," Blade wailed, his big chocolate-coloured eyes tearing up. "I tried to stop him."

"Cake," Flint supplied, unrepentant.

Mel looked over at the now mangled carrot cake on the side table.

Nate's suit was dotted with cream cheese fingerprints.

"God, I'm so sorry," Mel told him, "let me get a wet cloth."

"*No*." Nate's voice was sharp, then softer. "No, it's fine." His face, however, did not look like it was fine. "It will need dry-cleaning, I'm afraid. It's Armani."

Inside her head, Mel said a bad word.

~

Two hours later, Mel and Ellie finally said their last goodbyes, and shut the old oak door behind them. Mel leant against it and sighed.

"Right, I'll collect the glasses and bottles, you load the dishwasher and wipe down the tables." Ellie was all brisk efficiency. "But first I need to take off my shoes. My feet are killing me and I need a quick wee."

Mel looked pointedly at Ellie's feet. She was wearing ridiculously high, gold strappy stilettos.

"I know, I know, but you have to admit they make me look so much taller, and my calves look so good," Ellie laughed.

They were polar opposites really. Ellie was loud and brash

and colourful. She was also tiny and elfin-like. The two had been friends since they met in the halls during their first year of uni. Ellie came from a family of vintners and somme- liers. She'd grown up in Martinborough on a well-respected vineyard producing award-winning wines, gone to boarding school and had private cello lessons.

Melody, on the other hand, grew up a nomad with uncon- ventional parents. Geoff and Marion restored retro caravans these days, but as kids, she and Fern had lived in a house truck as part of a gypsy fair, on an angora goat farm for a year, spent eighteen months in Rarotonga growing produce for restaurants, and then on an old tug boat for most of her teen years. Money was always scarce. Clothes were home- made or recycled, and friendships hard to sustain.

But not with Ellie.

The idea for a bookstore that did wine and cheese eve- nings had been something they'd talked about since the first night they'd had drinks together.

Mel was the book lover. Ellie knew her wines. They were both foodies. Mel loved to bake and Ellie loved to eat. And they both bonded over their love of good cheese.

~

The dishes done, floors swept, and empty wine bottles put out in the recycling, they sat down on the antique chaise Marion had helped them restore, each with a glass of Malbec.

"To us," Mel toasted, putting her feet up on the coffee

table.

"And to George," Ellie added. "He would be so proud right now."

Mel looked up at the portrait of the scowling man hanging above the doorway. The one who'd made her dream a reality. She may have had too much to drink, or perhaps it was the sheen of tears, but she could have sworn he winked at her in the warm glow of the new bookstore.

Chapter two

"For what do we live, but to make sport for our neighbours, and laugh at them in our turn?"

Pride and Prejudice, Jane Austen

It was hard to decide if the thumping and banging was inside her head, or if an evil auctioneer had set up shop on her bedside table.

Mel pulled the pillow over her head with a groan. She was just drifting back to sleep when the sound of a buzz saw brought her rudely back from her failed attempt at sleeping in.

"For fuck's sake," she moaned, rolling over and cracking open an eye.

It was definitely early. Too early. Who the hell did construction on a Monday morning, at — she leant over and tapped her cellphone, the screen lit up and she squinted at the display — seven bloody am?

Christ almighty. It was her day off. Surely running power tools at that time of the morning was illegal, or at least extremely rude, she thought, flinging open the covers and getting out of her warm bed quickly before the draught made her reconsider.

She slid on her unicorn slippers and grabbed the closest jacket, a fur-lined trench coat she'd picked up at the second-hand store last winter.

Stomping down the narrow staircase and into the store, Mel nearly slid down her steps when the railing wobbled precariously. She opened the back door and set off down the street, scowling and muttering under her breath.

She'd only gone about a metre when she remembered the alarm, and shot back inside, only to realise she'd forgotten to set it last night before bed.

Back out into the street she went, past a white ute where a shaggy black dog sat up from the flat-bed and started to bark. Her head throbbed, and her stomach churned as she banged on the neighbouring door. She could hear someone singing to the radio, and the rhythmic sound of a nail gun popping. No one answered, so she turned the handle and went in.

A man stood with his broad back to her, wearing a worn grey T-shirt and faded jeans. His right arm had a tribal tattoo band and his thick brown hair curled out from under his hard hat. He was singing along, quite tunefully it had to be said, to Kenny Rogers' 'The Gambler' as he nailed Gib board along a wall.

"Excuse me," Mel croaked out, then cleared her throat and tried again. "Excuse me," she said loudly.

"You never count your money, when you're sittin' at the table—" he sang.

Melody tapped him on the shoulder and he shrieked. It was not a very manly sound. He spun around, hand over his heart. Mel's heart did a funny little jolt. He was quite attractive. Deep brown eyes, full lashes, and a chiselled jaw. If it wasn't for the hideous caterpillar-like moustache on his top lip, he'd be a total babe.

"Christ. You scared the crap out of me," he said a little breathlessly. He looked her up and down. A grin spread across his face as he took her in, and he did a snorty little laugh when his eyes reached her feet.

Mel had a little moment of regret. She realised belatedly that she had on her old 'Longest drink in town' T-shirt and her coat wasn't buttoned up. She should probably have taken the time to get dressed, she surmised. Still, she was not going to be deterred.

"There are people," she said forcefully, "who live here. And those people do *not* appreciate being woken up at some ungodly hour, by yobs with a big tool."

He let out a loud laugh and stopped when he saw her face. His lips moved from a grin to a thin line.

"Shit, I'm sorry," he said, "I really am. I didn't know there was anyone living nearby. I assumed it was all non-residential."

"Well, it's not," snapped Mel. She realised she was sounding like a total bitch, but she was hungover, tired and now that she thought about it, probably a bit premenstrual. "I'm right next door," she added. "And it's my first bloody day off in six weeks and you've ruined it."

"I really am sorry," he said, but his face had hardened up now, no sign of humour on it at all. "I'm just trying to do my job, and keep to a deadline. I'll make sure not to use any power tools till after eight."

"Fine," Mel said. "Thank you," she added belatedly, still sounding surly.

They stood in silence for a beat. A little standoff of sorts, neither one wanting to break eye contact. Her eyes narrowed. The furrow between his eyebrows deepened. No one spoke. Kenny had stopped singing and Freddy Mercury started up.

"Morning, boss, I got ya a coffee," called a voice down the hall. A young, scruffy-looking guy strolled in, tool belt clanging against his skinny thighs and his steel-capped boots shuffling through the sawdust, loud in the silence.

"Cheers, Skiddy," said the man. "I'm Jesse, by the way," he said to Mel, holding out a hand to her.

Mel reached across in an automatic reflex and took his hand. It was warm and calloused. She still couldn't seem to look away. The moment stretched awkwardly until he pulled back his hand and she added a little late "Mel. Nice to—" Nice to what though? She trailed off. "Anyway, thanks," she said limply before she turned and made her way back to the door, conscious of her slippers now and that her hair was probably a tangled nest. She hadn't brushed her teeth.

"Oh and Mel," Jesse called after her, "don't come back in here without a hard hat, okay?"

She slammed the door a little too hard on her way out, setting off the dog again as she went past. As she opened her front door she heard Jesse's voice yell out "SCRUBBER".

The cheek of him!

~

There didn't seem to be much point going back to bed. She was too wound up. Instead, she made herself a coffee and mopped the floor in the bookstore after she'd thrown in a batch of lemon and poppyseed muffins she wanted to trial.

The shop had been divided into two main rooms, the front having neat shelves of books and comfortable armchairs in pairs around low tables. Sun streamed through the large front window, and hopefully from the outside this would look like a cosy place to sit and read and while away the time. The U-shaped counter separated the front from the back section and this held tables and chairs and an artificial fire for those cooler Wellington evenings. A small industrial kitchen was located at the back and a door led to the hallway and the staircase up to Mel's flat.

~

Her muffins turned out pretty good and she was feeling marginally better after a shower and a couple of glasses of water when there was a knock at the front door.

It was Nate, dressed in chinos and a ribbed Henley, and carrying a large bunch of lilies which he presented to her after she let him in.

"Wow, you shouldn't have."

"I saw them, and I thought of you," Nate said, with his easy charm.

Lilies always made Mel think of funerals, but it was a lovely gesture.

"Actually, I'm glad you're here. I was planning to call you today. My stair banister is really loose, I think it may need replacing." She fumbled in the cupboard underneath the stairs looking for the vase she knew was in there. She had to pull out several bottles of her dad's home-made elderflower wine first. He had taken to bringing her a bottle of the bubbles every week, for her to serve in the shop. Mel didn't have the heart to tell him they weren't going to use them, and she couldn't bring herself to throw them out.

Finally, she located the box full of assorted bits and pieces she had salvaged from upstairs, after they had taken over from the previous owner. He had used the flat as a storage area for his bric-a-brac store 'Junk and Disorderly' and his hoarding had meant a major sort-out once they'd taken on the lease. She fished out a pewter vase and arranged the flowers while Nate checked out her stairs.

He came back and told her he'd get right onto someone to fix the railing. Her mind went straight to Jesse and she felt a small pang of regret that she'd been so shitty to him. Still, she told herself, he'd been no better.

Nate was leaning against the door frame, looking out the front window, and Mel was about to offer him a coffee when he announced he had to go, and shot off, saying he'd see her soon.

~

A few minutes later, Claire opened the door and stepped in, the bell jingling.

"Sorry, Claire, we're actually closed," Mel told her.

"I'm not here to buy anything," Claire scoffed. "It's about your rubbish."

Claire owned a small boutique clothing store across the road. She was slender and elegant with her hair in an immaculate chignon and wore red lipstick. Attractive in that English rose sort of way. Like she rode horses and did ballet as a child. She was also a complainer. Since Ellie and Mel had taken over the shop, she had done nothing but bitch and moan, from the colour they'd painted the front fretwork to customers lingering too long in the bookshop and taking up parking spaces.

"I don't mean to be critical," she began. Mel thought longingly of a hot bath and a paracetamol.

"But still, as a neighbourhood committee member, I feel it must be pointed out that there are regulations. Your copious liquor consumption could pose a problem. Not to mention I found a large amount of empty wine bottles in *my* recycling bin this morning."

Mel refrained from banging her head against the counter and started making another coffee.

"I'm sorry there were so many, Claire, but it really was a one-off incident. We finally had our opening night last night, but we don't anticipate anything like that sort of volume in a normal week. I am sorry we used your bin, but as yours was empty, and since the truck was coming this morning, we thought it better to use yours rather than a cardboard box that they might miss. It won't happen again."

Claire sniffed.

"Well, see that it doesn't," she said. "I don't appreciate being labelled a drinker when I most certainly am not."

"Sorry," Mel repeated. "Can I make you a coffee?"

She hoped Claire would decline.

"A skinny chai latte for me," Claire requested as she looked around the store.

Mel and Ellie had spent hours cleaning and decorating and were ridiculously proud of the result. They'd polished the brass light fittings, sanded and oiled the wood floors, and carefully put together a look like an old-fashioned library. They thought the comfortable upholstered seats, mismatched tea cups and side tables gave it a warm, inviting feel. From the frown on Claire's face, Mel thought she might not agree.

They sat at one of the back tables where they served drinks and nibbles. Coffee and cake during the day, and wine and cheese in the afternoon and at night. They made awkward small talk for a bit, which consisted mainly of Mel asking about Claire's boutique. Claire announced she had to go, as she had so much to do. Like Mel had been the one to impose on her. As she left, she noticed the lilies on the side table.

"Lovely flowers. I adore lilies. My boyfriend buys them for me all the time. Such a classic, timeless bloom."

Mel contemplated telling her to take them. The smell wasn't helping her hangover, but they did look nice and it would seem ungracious to regift them. She wondered briefly what sort of man Claire would date. Investment banker, she imagined. Maybe balding. Money for sure.

"Have a nice day," she told her neighbour, closing the door behind her and locking it.

As she looked out the window, she noticed Jesse getting into the cab of the ute. He glanced her way and she quickly ducked down so he wouldn't catch her looking. She felt like a weird cat burglar or a bumbling spy. Pathetic, she told herself. She pretended to be checking under the chairs for any stray crackers to make herself feel like less of a loser, before getting up and heading upstairs. She didn't look back.

She was going back to bed to read her book.

Chapter three

"I do not wish to avoid the walk. The distance is nothing when one has a motive."

Pride and Prejudice, Jane Austen

When Mel opened the shop the next morning she wasn't surprised to find Olive outside waiting for her to open. Olive shrugged off her drab beige coat and hung it on the rack. It was there for this exact purpose; in the hope that customers would feel comfortable and free to spend as much time in the shop as they wished.

Tuesday was Olive's day off and she spent the entire morning in the bookshop, sitting in the same seat each week, reading contentedly. At 10am she would sigh and put down whatever book she was reading carefully on the side table and say to Mel: "I think I'll have a pot of tea. Maybe one of those scones [or muffins or whatever sweet treat Mel had made that morning] as well, thank you." Olive was a creature of habit.

Over the weeks that she'd been coming in, Mel had discovered that Olive worked in a rest home and rented a room in Kelburn. She was trained as a bookkeeper, but had left the work when her own mother got sick and went into care. Mel suspected she was lonely and had few, if any, friends.

It was hard to pick Olive's age. She was such an old-fashioned dresser, with her hair always pulled back into a tight bun, and her face could have placed her at anywhere between twenty-five and forty. But Mel guesstimated, from things she had said, that she was possibly closest to thirty.

They had taken to chatting for a bit when she arrived, often about books. Olive was amazingly well read on a huge range of topics. She came alive, Mel thought, when she talked about literature. She knew all the classics and new releases but was also a reader of some surprising genres, like science fiction and horror. Mel was more a romance, historical fiction and classics kind of girl.

Mel had just removed the tray with the empty teapot when Ellie bustled in.

"Morning, Olive, nice weekend?"

"Yes, thank you, Ellie. I bought myself a long-handled duster and caught up on a bit of spring cleaning. Is it sad that that was the highlight of my weekend?" she laughed. "I finally managed to get the cobwebs from the high corners of my room though. Those older houses can be difficult to keep spick and span, can't they?"

"I imagine so." Ellie lived with her friend Geri in a trendy, light-filled apartment and wouldn't have it any other way. She'd been quite happy for Mel, who had been alternating sleeping on Ellie's sofa and at her parents' house during the renovation, to have the dingy little flat above the bookstore.

"I've just been to that new organic wine shop in town," she told Mel, placing a box on the counter. "Bought a few to try out this week. And look at this." With a flourish she pulled an emerald-green blouse, decorated with oversized fuchsia buttons, out of a carrier bag. "Is this not stunning? Mirror Mirror just got some new stock in. I've got my eye on a gorgeous pair of boots too. Might go back later and try them on."

Ellie plucked a lemon poppyseed muffin from the counter and plopped herself down at the nearest table.

"These are good," she mumbled, through a mouthful of crumbs. "Many customers?"

"Just Olive, so far." Tuesday mornings were always a bit slow. Later, they'd probably get a few people come in on their lunch break, or English Lit students from the university passing time on their way to an afternoon lecture. "Did you pick up the post on your way back?"

"Damn, forgot, sorry, I'll grab it tomorrow. You weren't expecting anything, were you?"

"Nothing that can't wait."

"I'm going to do a stocktake for Wednesday night." Ellie

pulled herself up reluctantly from her chair, and swept the crumbs from her muffin into a small, neat pile and into her hand. The bookstore had been open for a couple of months but this was the first week for the cheese and wine and they were both excited to see how it would go. How it would be accepted by the community. If Sunday's opening was anything to go by, they both thought it would do pretty well. They had decided they would do Wednesday through to Saturday nights to start with. Mel had also put a post on their social media and web pages for a monthly book club.

At eleven forty-five Olive stood, sighed happily and brought the current book to the counter to purchase.

"See you next week," she said. "Good luck with the wine side of things." As she was leaving the shop, Marion stepped through the door.

Mel gave her a smile. Her mother really was the ultimate hippie. Today she wore a tie-dyed mumu with Birkenstocks. She smelt like sandalwood and was carrying a large, flat parcel, wrapped in brown butcher's paper. Whatever the occasion, Marion would wrap it in plain, brown, recycled paper.

"Sweetpea," she leant over to peck Mel on the cheek. "As promised, I've brought you a special piece of artwork. I'm sure it'll be snapped up in no time, but never fear, there will be plenty more to follow."

"I didn't think I actually agreed to sell your work," Mel

said, but her mother flapped a hand dismissively and handed the painting over.

"Nonsense. Remember how we were saying those walls are crying out for a bit of colour? Well, go on then. Unwrap it."

Mel tentatively removed the paper from the painting. Very bold, it featured a pale-pink background with a bulbous red oval, shades of darker pink in the middle.

"Err — it's — what is it exactly?"

"I call it 'Lady Flower'. Because of the colours." Marion beamed proudly.

Mel raised the painting higher to get a better look. She stared in horror.

"Good Lord. It looks like a vagina."

"Rubbish. Obviously it's been a long time since you've seen a vagina if you think that. I'd suggest you buy yourself a hand mirror."

There was a choking sound behind Mel as Ellie came back in from the storeroom.

"It's very colourful, Marion. Mel, I think you might be holding it upside down."

Mel flipped the painting over but it didn't seem to make much improvement and her mother's swirly signature definitely indicated she'd had it right the first time.

Marion was glancing around the room, as if contemplating the best wall for her masterpiece. Mel put the painting down firmly behind the counter. "I'll need to get some picture hooks, but I'll have to do that later. What brings you to town?"

"Fern's asked me to pick the boys up but I thought I'd pop in and see you first. And I need to buy some more art supplies. Your poor sister, she's just exhausted. I'm going to cook them a nice dhal for dinner. God knows those kids could do with a few nutrients other than those junk-laden snacks she lets them have."

To be fair to Fern, Marion considered anything processed or most sugar-based things to be junk. As kids she had insisted they only have honey to sweeten anything and the girls' biggest treat was an oat slice that had cacao nibs in it. They were the weird kids who thought cauliflower pizza was normal. Marion had eased up a lot over the years, but she was still a bit judgmental when it came to Mel and Fern's eating habits.

Mel personally thought that her sister had plenty of time to herself as the boys were at school all week and she didn't work. Although the younger one, Flint, was a bit of a handful, he was hilarious and Blade was a gorgeous, sweet-natured and sensitive wee boy.

"I was thinking I could do a wine and painting evening sometime, Melly," Marion said. "I'm sure it would be a hit, and I'd be happy to act as tutor. It's wonderful to see people shed their inhibitions and discover a more creative side."

She was saved from answering by Ellie.

"That's a lovely idea, Marion, but I really don't think we have the space. I'm sure you'd need quite a bit of room to achieve that level of expression."

Mel shot Ellie a grateful look.

"Well, maybe later, when things are a bit more established," Marion said. "I'm trying my hand at sculpture at the moment and I must say, I really think it could be my thing."

It would have been unkind to point out that everything her mother tried was 'her thing' at first; from macramé pot-holders in the late seventies, rag-rolling walls in the nineties and more recently she'd even done a graffiti art workshop.

"Your father and I had a lovely time at the opening." Marion folded the wrapping paper from the painting and carefully put it into her string shopping bag. "Geoff suggested you could give him that book he was reading for Christmas. He might possibly have got a little bit of cake on it."

"I'll put it aside," Mel said. "Anyone want coffee?"

"Love one, I didn't have time this morning," Ellie said.

Marion waggled her eyebrows. "Where were you this morning, Ellie? Coming home from a hot date maybe?"

"I wish, Marion. The only person I'm dating at the moment is myself, I'm afraid."

"Nothing wrong with a bit of self-love, darling. Everyone does it, nothing to be ashamed of."

"Mum ..."

"Yes, sweetheart? And what about you? Are you seeing anyone at the moment? I thought Nate was lovely. Perhaps you should ask him out?"

When her mother finally left, Mel sank down with a groan.

Ellie pulled the painting out from behind the counter and studied it closely, her head tilted to the side.

"You're right, it does look very vagina-like," she said finally. "What should we do with it?"

"It's not staying here, that's for sure."

"Hmmm, I don't know," Ellie laughed. "Perhaps Colin would be interested in buying it. Poor misguided man. He might think you'd modelled it."

Mel swatted her on the arm. "Stop it. Don't encourage him. Anyway, if you had a hand mirror, Ellie, you'd find your girly bits looked nothing like that, according to my mother."

She picked the painting up and took it out the back.

"It's going in the dumpster and I'll tell Marion I sold it."

Ellie grinned. "I'd pay someone fifty bucks to sneak into Claire's shop and nail it to her wall."

They both laughed at the thought of the immaculate and rather snobbish Claire discovering such a vulgar painting hanging in her tasteful little shop.

A wine rep came in then to see Ellie, followed by two customers, so they both wandered into the main part of the shop.

Mel breathed in the smell of new books and floor polish and

again glanced up at the portrait of George Henry, as she did several times a day. She'd worked for George for years, organising both his professional and personal life, particularly once the Parkinson's had got to the stage that he could no longer type himself. He'd never lost his brilliance, in her opinion, although his mind had definitely taken a more rambling path and the poems and stories he'd written in those last couple of years some people considered quite bizarre.

George was still a well-respected writer to the very end though. He had many colleagues and academics who sought his company but few people he called friends. He hadn't left the house for the last six months of his life.

Many times he'd tested Mel's patience and she'd threatened to quit, particularly when she was down on her hands and knees scrubbing the kitchen floor or being sent on a wild goose chase to hunt down a particularly rare brand of whisky, but she'd been fond of the grumpy old bugger. It turned out he was fond of her too. George had no family, and he'd left her enough money in his will for her to fund her share in the shop. They'd named it Pinot and Pūhā, after George's best-known novel.

Many people believed George's death was a hunting accident. Mel knew otherwise.

"If I ever get fed up enough with all this shit, I'm bloody well going to go bush and shoot myself," he'd told her once. "Now make me a batch of those cheese scones, won't you? You didn't give me any bloody lunch."

That was exactly what had happened. After not leaving the house once for months, and almost driving her crazy with it, she'd got up one morning to find him gone. The Jeep wasn't in the garage, his green hunting beanie and jacket were missing from the coat rack (the same one she now had in the shop) and his gun was gone from the safe. George's body had been found a week later, deep in the Tararua ranges. The TV and newspapers had been full of the story for a while, followed by memorial tributes and even a TV documentary about his life. George would have hated it.

"Excuse me," a customer said, and Mel turned to the woman with a helpful smile.

Chapter four

*"There are few people whom I really love
and still fewer of whom I think well."*

Pride and Prejudice, Jane Austen

Wednesday was generally a good day for the shop and that night would officially be the first evening they were open. Mel had organised a local Wellington author to come in to do a reading and she was hoping this would bring in more customers. She was just arranging the new book *Into the Bright Space* attractively on the central display shelf when Fern arrived.

"Hi, sis, got time to make me a coffee?"

Not really, Mel thought, but pushed herself up from the floor and led her sister into the middle part of the shop, going behind the counter to the coffee machine.

"So, how are the boys?" she asked, tamping down the coffee grounds and taking a cup from the neatly stacked pile.

"A pain, as usual. Honestly, Mel, you have *no* idea what it's like. You're so lucky you don't have kids. Some days I wish I had an easy life like you."

Mel said nothing. She put the coffee down in front of Fern as well as a cheese and caramelised onion scone. She'd learnt by now there was no point disagreeing with Fern, who was three years younger but acted like she knew everything. Besides, Mel was not even thirty; she didn't feel like she was in any hurry to have children, unlike Fern who had had Blade after a brief fling when she was eighteen. The dad hadn't stuck around. Neither had Flint's.

Fern stirred sugar into her coffee and took a bite of the scone, immediately pulling a face. "Ew, what is this? It tastes gross. Don't you have anything else? And your coffee tastes off too. Did you clean the machine properly?"

"I have blueberry slice but it's still cooling," Mel replied, but didn't offer to get her any. "So, what's up?"

Fern sighed and crumbled the scone unnecessarily all over the plate. Mel had to stop herself from swooping in and picking the crumbs up from the floor as they dropped.

"Can you have the boys for me Saturday night? I really need a night off and Chase is being an arse about having them."

"It'll be our first Saturday we're open, sorry. I can't really keep an eye on them and be down here as well."

"Won't Ellie be here? She can look after all this." Fern

waved an arm dismissively.

"No, sorry."

"Sunday then? Please, Mel. Just for the evening even? The boys love to spend time with their aunty. Blade's been begging me and he's written a special story for you."

Mel's heart melted and she capitulated.

"All right, but don't bring them too early, okay? We're open until four."

"Cool, thanks." Fern leapt up and grabbed her bag, a lumpy pink, vinyl thing, from the floor where she'd dumped it. "Gotta go, things to see, people to do an' all that."

"See you on Sunday then," Mel called, and Fern gave her a wave and was gone, leaving her still full coffee cup and crumbs everywhere.

Mel finished arranging the books for that night and was scanning a pile of new arrivals into the computer when Colin poked his head around the door.

"Good afternoon, fair neighbour."

"Hello, Colin, how are you today?" Mel replied politely, swallowing back the sigh that always threatened to escape when she saw him. "I'm afraid the book you ordered hasn't arrived yet."

"Not to worry, not to worry. I thought I might trouble you for a cup of tea. Peppermint, please. Excellent for the digestion."

Mel took his proffered keep-cup, not wanting to point out that she was sure he had a perfectly fine kitchenette at his own business. A customer was a customer, she told herself. She made the tea and then politely excused herself to help a woman who was looking for a book for her grandson.

~

Under the glass counter, Mel had what she considered her only, and most prized, possession. As kids, they grew up with parents who despised materialism, and it was certainly a trait that had stuck. Mel would rather spend her money on doing rather than owning things, until the shop. But she had one object that she loved above all else and that was her copy of *Pinot and Pūhā*. It was a first edition copy and George had gruffly given it to her, saying something along the lines of "Here, I suppose you'll want one of these."

Inside he'd addressed it to her and signed it with a little note that read 'You're very bearable.'

Olive had noticed it the first week they opened and Mel had taken it out to show her. Olive had handled the book carefully and reverently and grinned when she read the inscription.

"I imagine that's high praise from him," she noted. Mel had felt quite teary about it all over again.

Today, she got it out to dust it and then carefully put it back, hoping George was proud of her and the shop, and feeling grateful for having had him in her life.

Thursday, Mel got up early and walked down to the local yoga studio for an Ashtanga session. When she got back to the shop, her parents were there. Luckily, the rubbish collection had come and gone and Marion's awful painting along with it.

She let them in, and set about making hot drinks.

Her mother often popped by unexpectedly, but it was rarer for her father to visit for no reason. He had another bottle of wine with him that he handed over as he hugged her.

"How are you, Melly?" her mother asked. "Have you taken that sexy landlord for a test run yet?"

"Mum, it's not normal to ask your child that," Mel sighed.

"Nonsense, it's healthy to talk about sex, and anyway, who wants to be normal?" Marion told her.

Me, sometimes, Mel thought, but she stayed quiet. "How are you guys?" she asked instead.

"Good, good. Busy. We might go to a beatbox class at the community centre next weekend," Marion said.

"We just wanted to pop in and give you some news," Geoff added.

"What's up?" Mel asked. "And please don't say Fern's pregnant again," she joked.

The joke fell flat. There was an ominous silence.

"No! She's not!"

Her mother sighed. "I know I've always told you girls that

it wasn't important to be married, and that children came when you were ready for them, but I have to admit I really did think Fern might have more sense than this."

Mel looked at her father. He looked back and shrugged. "She's a slow learner, it would seem."

Bloody hell.

"How far along is she?"

"Um, a few months, I think," said Marion vaguely.

"Too far," Geoff muttered under his breath, making Mel snort her coffee.

The door chimed as Ellie entered.

"Morning," said Ellie, "Hello, Marion, Geoff, you're here early."

"You know us, Ellie, always up early. Best time of the day," Geoff said. "I'm sure Marion and I were both larks in a previous life."

"Goodness, what is the time?" Marion said with a start. "We don't want to be late for the therapist."

"Therapist?" Mel asked. "Why are you seeing a therapist? What's wrong?"

The thought that her parents were having relationship trouble was alarming. While other people's parents had grown apart, Mel's always claimed they'd grown closer together over the years.

"Oh, nothing's wrong, sweetie, it's a sex therapist. Dad and I are keen to explore the concept of a more tantric experience. Sort of like edging, but with intimacy. You don't need to see a therapist only when something's wrong, darling."

Mel wished she hadn't asked. That mental picture was going to last far too long. She may need a therapist herself.

She told Ellie about Fern as they went over the accounts and wrote a few lists. Ellie tended to do all the bookwork for the shop and the wine and cheese ordering while Mel did the coffee and food side.

"Beggar for punishment, isn't she?" Ellie noted wryly.

"Yep," Mel agreed, "and she has a type, that's for sure — and it's not reliable. I doubt Chase will be any different."

~

That afternoon, as they were prepping for the night, a customer came out of the bathroom and discreetly told Mel there seemed to be a bit of a puddle on the floor.

Mel thanked her for letting her know, and promptly forgot about it until after she'd served several customers, and needed a wee herself.

When she opened the bathroom door, it was more like a small flood.

Ellie had gone to pick up some fresh bread, and Mel couldn't think what to do.

The water gurgled out from a soggy mess of plaster at the side of the toilet. Where the hell was it coming from? The only thing on the other side of the wall was the new art gallery that was being renovated. Shit. It must be something to do with the builders, she thought. That bloody arsehole.

She turned the closed sign on the store, and strode down the footpath to find Jesse.

Chapter five

"Angry people are not always wise."

Pride and Prejudice, Jane Austen

"For fuck's sake, one of you lot get the water turned off. Hoppy, call Mark and see if he can get over here to look at the pipes. Skiddy, you bloody meathead, I'm gonna fucking gut you if this has fucked the floor."

Jesse, it seemed, had also discovered the leak. Water sprayed out in an arc from the wall. People were frantically moving saws and other tools and Jesse was soaked. His white top was transparent, dripping wet. He was quite the sight, Mel had to admit. When he turned and saw her, his scowling face looked murderous.

"What the hell did I say about wearing a hard hat?" he yelled. "Skiddy, get some brooms in here and move some of this water, and Len, see if you can pull the wall back without fucking the skirting."

Jesse strode towards her as he spoke and Mel found herself at a loss for words until he was standing directly in front of her. He looked like he was posing for a fireman's calendar, all manly and buff.

"Are you bloody deaf?" he shouted. "Get the hell out." He reached out, turning Mel roughly by her shoulders and pushed her out the open door onto the footpath.

"It's not safe to enter a building site without a hat." He seemed livid.

Water dripped off the side of his moustache, and suddenly he wasn't so attractive, Mel thought.

"Well, I wouldn't need to come over here *again*," she shouted, "except that your drama is causing an unwanted swimming pool in my shop. Also, you clearly have an anger problem. You really need to sort that out."

She knew she sounded like a banshee, but there was something about Jesse that just rubbed her up the wrong way.

"Bloody hell." Jesse wearily rubbed a large hand over his chin. He took a deep breath in. Then out.

"Sorry, it's a burst pipe. And these old buildings often share water mains. I've hopefully got a plumber coming, and the water should be off now, so I'll come by as soon as I get a minute and take a look, okay?"

"Great, just great," Mel said. "And what am I supposed to do till you decide to pop in for a look? Put on my bikini?"

Jesse opened his mouth and then shut it again. He did the

breathing thing again. "Go for it, sweetheart. I'm sure that's a sight. Or maybe find a mop," he scowled. "Anyway, that's the best I can do right now."

There was a tense silence as they both looked daggers at each other.

Mel broke eye contact first, looking down at his torso, only to see that his well-defined abs were visible against the soaked top. She felt herself blushing so she blurted out "See that you do" in a weird school-marmish tone, and took off.

That hadn't even made sense, she lamented again as she wrung sopping wet towels into a bucket. What a bloody day.

The bell chimed again. She'd left the closed sign on, so hoped it was Ellie or Jesse. It was Nate in another expensive-look-ing suit and Mel became aware that her pants were soaked at the knees and her hair had come out of its tidy bun. She probably looked a wreck, she thought.

"Nate, hi." She tried to sound pleased to see him. But real-ly, as her landlord, he should technically be giving her notice before he turned up, shouldn't he? Still, if he was here about the railing, she could ask him about an insurance claim for the cost of repairs for the flood too.

"Hello, beautiful, what's happened here? I wondered why you were closed."

"Burst pipe next door," Mel told him. "It's leaked through the old weatherboards unfortunately."

"Right, that's a shame. Still, I'm sure it's all fixable. Now I was—"

"Shit. What happened?" Ellie had come through and set a shopping bag on the counter.

"Burst pipe next door," Mel repeated. "It's flooded the loo. I've got most of the water out now."

"Is that why the plumber's outside?" Ellie asked, taking the towel from Mel and throwing it in the bucket as Mel stood.

"I think he's here for Jesse," Mel told her. "The builder next door," she explained when Ellie looked blank.

"Right," Ellie nodded. "Coffee, Nate?"

"Oh yes, thanks." Nate gave her a wink. "Love a flat white."

Mel tried to fix up her hair a bit. "Actually, you can't. The water's off. So, Nate, are you here about the railing?"

Nate helped himself to a scone from under the cloche and looked questioningly at Mel. "Railing?"

"The one on my stairs?" Mel reminded him. "You were going to get it fixed."

"Right, right, the railing." Nate smiled and looked a bit sheepish, pulling out a chair and taking a seat. "Sorry, I'll make some calls ASAP. Just been flat out, you know, ..." He trailed off as he bit into the scone, chewed and swallowed.

"Actually, Mel, I was here to see if you wanted to get dinner. I know a great, exclusive little place on Cuba Street. Asian fusion. Chef's a mate of mine actually and I thought we could go?"

Mel looked up as the bell rang again for the door. It seemed the closed sign wasn't a deterrent.

"Hey, Mel? It's Jesse. Um, the builder. I've got the plumber with me ..."

Jesse appeared in the doorway and surveyed the scene. He'd taken off his hard hat and his hair was flat on top but a curly mass at the bottom. When he saw Nate, his face went from a tentative smile back to his thunderous scowl. Nate, for his part, looked oddly jumpy.

"Mel, this is Mark, the plumber." He indicated a tall skinny guy in overalls. "Mind if we just assess the damage?"

Ellie leapt off the counter where she was perched. "It's in the loo," she told him. "I'll show you, I want to look myself."

The three of them went down the hall and into the cubicle.

Mel smiled at Nate. "I have to work most nights, sorry," she told him. She looked at the mess around her. "Although perhaps not tonight," she mused.

Down the hall, she heard Jesse ask Ellie, "How the hell do you know that jumped-up git?"

How rude. If she'd heard, Nate surely had too. She smiled awkwardly at him.

"I can book it for later?" he suggested. "Give you time to sort some stuff. And anyway, no one who's anyone goes out before nine."

The group returned back to the room at that point and Jesse gave Nate another glare.

"Well, that sounds great," Mel said more enthusiastically

than she really felt. "I'd love to have dinner, thank you."

There was a short silence until Ellie blurted out "Oh piss off, Claire."

She was looking out the window at their neighbour marching across the road towards them.

Nate got up and brushed down his suit.

"Well, great, Mel, I'll just have a quick look at that railing and let myself out the back. Shall I pick you up, or meet you there?"

Mel was feeling a little flustered. She wasn't sure why he needed another look at the railing. And Jesse was staring at her. "Oh, umm, I'll meet you," she suggested.

"Great, great, nine o'clock at the fountain on Cuba then?" He disappeared abruptly out the back as Claire arrived.

"Ladies. There seems to be a large service vehicle parked in my spot."

"Sorry, love, that's mine," Mark said, "but I'll be out of ya hair in a jiffy." He turned to Jesse. "I'll be back first thing with the fittings for next door, mate."

"Cheers, Mark, appreciate the quick service," Jesse told him. They shook hands before he left.

Claire sniffed. "The fact remains, that car park is for my customers and having work vans parked outside my boutique lowers the tone considerably."

"The parking isn't allocated at all, Claire," Ellie told her. "So it's not *your* park."

"Just see that it doesn't happen again," Claire said, basically ignoring the logic. She wrinkled her nose and pursed her lips into a little moue of distaste. "Although I would appreciate it if you wouldn't give food to that homeless man. You're just encouraging him to keep hanging around, you know."

The homeless man was Kevin. Mel had taken to giving him leftover baking. She often saw him, his old overcoat pulled around himself, slumped in the doorway of the dry-cleaning shop next to Claire's. He was always gone early the next morning.

Without waiting for a reply, Claire turned and flounced out.

"Silly bitch," said Ellie.

Mel looked at Jesse who was watching Claire's retreating arse. "That was actually your fault," she told him acidly. "Again."

He turned and contemplated her for a bit. Then he directed his comments pointedly at Ellie. "So, the damage is only superficial by the looks of it, luckily. I'll bring in a heater to dry out the wall cavity overnight and I'll have someone come over and replaster it for you in the morning." He looked over at Mel. "Not too early of course," he said. "Nice to meet *you*, Ellie."

And with that, he left.

Arsehole.

"He's kinda hot," Ellie noted.

Mel just huffed in reply.

Chapter six

"It is often nothing but our own vanity that deceives us."

Pride and Prejudice, Jane Austen

True to his word, Jesse brought an industrial fan over to dry up the water, setting it up and leaving without a word. By the time Mel and Ellie had cleaned up the mess, the last thing Mel felt like doing was going out for dinner.

She felt a bit bummed about having to close for the evening too, especially so early on, and hoped any potential customers would be understanding.

Ellie left and Mel locked the door behind her, having attached a neatly written note explaining the 'unforeseen circumstances' that meant they were unexpectedly closed. She made her way upstairs to shower, only remembering when she turned the tap that the water was off. Great.

The only person Mel knew who lived nearby was Claire

and there was no way she was going to ask her if she could use her shower, so she went into the kitchen and switched on the kettle, which was thankfully full. She'd have to wash her pits and bits and hope that was enough. A good spray of perfume and extra lick of deodorant should help too, she thought.

Exactly how fancy was this 'exclusive' little restaurant? What Mel really felt like was a cheese toastie and a cup of tea. Sighing, she picked out a black and red patterned knee-length dress, a black blazer and a pair of strappy black shoes. She brushed her hair out and twisted it into a knot, fastening it with a clip, hoping it would hold out and wasn't too limp and sweaty from cleaning. They'd been so busy getting the shop ready for opening and dealing with all the minor hic-cups that come with running a small business that she hadn't been out in weeks. Really, she should be looking forward to a night out, but frankly, Mel was just as happy at home with a book and something simple she'd cooked herself.

Looking longingly back at her comfy bed she went down the stairs, carefully avoiding the rickety banister, to meet the Uber.

Nate was waiting at the bucket fountain on Cuba Street, standing far enough away to be sure he wouldn't get splashed. He wore a different suit than earlier; this one navy blue and slim fitting. He wore it with a pink shirt slightly open at the neck, his hands casually in the pockets, looking suave. His blond hair was brushed back almost in a quiff and he looked Mel up and down as she approached. "You look lovely." He linked an arm through hers.

Two young ladies walking past gave Nate an appreciative look and giggled into their hands, whispering to each other. He did look handsome, Mel thought, and she liked a man who could dress well.

The restaurant had only been open a few months and was proving popular, Nate told her as they walked. Mel had, of course, heard about it. Wellington was a small city and there was always a buzz when somewhere new opened.

"It's pretty hard to get a table, especially at the last minute. They're usually fully booked, but lucky for you I have connections." He gave her a wink.

Mai-Kai was tiny, and beautifully decorated with polished ebony tables and oyster-coloured silk lanterns. The walls were hung with moody-looking photos of vivid-green paddy fields and mist-shrouded villages. The half dozen or so tables were intimately placed with ornate dividers between them so that the diners almost felt like they were in an up-market private home.

As Mel studied the menu, she tried not to choke at the prices. It certainly made their cheeseboards look like good value. Hopefully the food was delicious and not just pretentious, like it sounded.

Nate waved a hand expansively. "Have whatever you feel

like, don't stress about the cost, darling."

"I'm really not that hungry," Mel murmured. There was
that 'darling' endearment again.

The efficient waiter gave them just the right amount of
time after bringing their drinks — a lovely bottle of Pinot
Gris Nate had chosen that was excessively overpriced — before discreetly appearing at the table to take their order.

As he left, Nate reached across and took Mel's hand. She
was aware that her nails were unpolished and one had broken in the clean-up that afternoon. After a few seconds, she
slid her hand away from his to pick up her wine glass. Hand
holding was more second date territory, Mel thought.

"It's nice to have such charming tenants," he told her,
topping up her glass with a smile.

"Do you own other buildings?" Mel asked him, curious. He
looked to be no older than her but, if you could judge by the
way he dressed, seemed to be doing well for himself.

"A few, but let's not talk shop right now. I've been looking
forward to getting to know you better." He swirled the wine
in his glass and sipped it. "Ever since you signed the lease,
actually. You kind of remind me of a hot librarian we had
at school."

"Did you grow up around here?" Mel asked him, searching
to change the topic. He'd probably meant to compliment her
but it had the opposite effect.

"Yes, my family are very well known in Wellington," he
said, "but my parents live on the Gold Coast now. They're

retired. I manage their property portfolio. As well as my own properties of course," he added hastily.

"That must be interesting," Mel replied politely.

"Yes, very interesting, but hugely challenging." Nate gave her a wry smile. "Of course it helps if you're well connected. My godfather is Sir Wesley Powell."

Mel looked at him blankly.

"Investment banker?"

"I've only lived here since uni."

"Of course. Sorry, I don't mean to bore you. Sir Wesley was a huge name back in the eighties. I'm surprised you haven't heard of him though. You'll find plenty of information on him on the internet." The waiter approached with the first of their dishes, which steamed aromatically. "Ah, here's our food."

The food tasted amazing, though Mel didn't think it was good value at all. Tiny plates beautifully presented but you could easily leave hungry. Luckily Nate had ordered plenty.

"So you went to university here too?" she asked as she manoeuvred a perfectly caramelised scallop with her chopsticks, hoping she wouldn't drop it before it got to her mouth.

Nate seemed to consider his answer. "Partly. I did a couple of years of a commerce degree here but I really wanted to get out of Wellington for a bit, so I moved to Auckland. Dad set me up in business there for a while. I've been back here now for a couple of years."

Nate gallantly offered Mel the last dumpling, but she

declined.

"Your family is obviously supportive of your business." He dabbed his lips carefully with his napkin. "It was nice they all showed up in force for your opening evening."

"They're very supportive," she agreed. "My parents have always encouraged my sister and me to follow our dreams and to do what makes us happy. They've spent their own lives doing exactly that. I guess they were a little unconventional for their time; never marrying, much to my grandparents' dismay, and home-schooling us for the main part."

"And yet you went to university?"

Mel laughed. "Yes. Home-schooled kids can go on to tertiary education, you know. I majored in English Literature. I have a masters, in fact. Do you have brothers or sisters?"

"Only child. Probably a bit spoiled, to be fair," he laughed. "The whole stereotype."

Mel knew about stereotypes. As well as being hippies and nomads, her parents had brought them up vegan. She wasn't any longer: she liked good cheese too much and she was pretty sure Fern's favourite food was a McDonald's Quarter Pounder these days.

They had finished eating and Mel stifled a yawn. "That was lovely, but I really must get home. The builders will probably turn up at the crack of dawn to fix that wall."

Nate fiddled with his fancy watch. "So, that builder guy, Jesse did he say his name was? How well do you know him?"

"Know him? I don't know him at all. He seems to be the

guy in charge next door and so far, all he's been is rude and arrogant."

"Typical tradesman. Probably best you try to avoid him as much as possible. He looks like trouble to me. Have you got to know many of the other business owners in the block?"

Mel had every intention of avoiding Jesse, but not because she had anything against tradesmen. Her issue was more a personal dislike of boorish and inconsiderate people.

"A few, but not well yet. They all seemed pleased to have the bookshop open but a couple of them haven't been as happy about us opening at night."

In truth, Claire was the only one who had a problem with this, perhaps because she also lived above her shop but Mel wasn't about to point fingers.

Their waiter arrived with the bill.

"Please, let me get this," Nate insisted.

"Shall we go halves?" Mel asked. She wasn't entirely happy having him pay for her meal, although she wasn't exactly sure why she felt so strongly about this. Perhaps because he was her landlord, or because her parents had always taught her to be independent. Maybe it was just that he made her feel slightly uncomfortable. She didn't like the thought that he might feel she 'owed' him.

"No, I insist," Nate was saying. "I've enjoyed your company and I do want you to be able to pay the rent, after all." He laughed after he'd said this, not seeming to notice Mel didn't find the comment at all funny.

Nate was patting his pockets, making a bit of a show of it.

"Oh bugger it." More patting. "I seem to have left my wallet behind. This is really embarrassing."

Mel pulled out her credit card. "That's okay, I can get it." As she slipped the card into the receipt folder she glanced at the bill and gulped. Being a new business owner, she was normally quite frugal and this wasn't the kind of place she'd have chosen to eat. It was more a special occasion restaurant, reserved for birthdays and anniversaries, those kinds of events. The city was full of great places to eat with more reasonable prices. But Nate looked like a 'see and be seen' type of guy, she reflected.

"Are you sure? I'll pay you back." Nate sat back with a wry smile. "Actually, do you know Evan Moon, the actor? I was good friends with him at school and he has a movie premiere soon. Maybe I could take you? I could probably wrangle a meet and greet at the end if you like?"

Mel had heard of the movie. It was a sci-fi thing, not really her favourite genre. She gave Nate what she hoped was a non-committal answer.

"Coffee?" he asked her, when they were outside. "I live nearby if you—"

"I'd really better get home," Mel replied, taking a step away from him in case he felt the need to kiss her goodnight. "The builders and — well — Friday's a busy day for us."

Nate looked disappointed, but shrugged, looking at his watch. "I guess I'll see you soon then."

"Sure, thanks for a nice evening."

He gave her an awkward little salute and Mel did a brief wave in return, heading in the opposite direction. He hasn't even thanked me for the very expensive dinner, she thought begrudgingly.

Chapter seven

"... 'Keep your breath to cool your porridge'..."

Pride and Prejudice, Jane Austen

Mel woke up feeling grumpy. She'd only had five hours' sleep, there was no hot water for a shower and she'd put cornflour in her brownie mix instead of baking powder. She had to start again.

She'd also straightened her hair, and put on more make-up than usual and was a little irked at herself for it. So what if Jesse kept seeing her at her worst, it's not like she fancied the man. I mean, physically he was her type, sure, but his personality was not at all appealing. And it wasn't even likely it would be him that came to fix her wall this morning anyway.

After she fixed the hot water fuse, she made herself a juice and put in some toast, then waited for her batch of brownies

to cool and tried to find her usual good humour. As she unlocked the front door, she noticed Kevin getting up to leave
his spot. She gave him a wave to catch his attention and
called him over.

There were a few bran muffins left from yesterday so she
put them in a bag for him, along with an apple and went out
to meet him. Part of her hoped Claire would see, as a bit of
an 'up yours, Claire'. Kevin gave her a grateful smile and meandered off, patting the dog on Jesse's ute as he went past.
She wondered where he went during the day. Maybe she'd
ask her mum if she had any of their old camping gear still. A
sleeping bag would be good, she thought.

"You all good if I come do your wall now?" a voice said
next to her, and she jumped in surprise.

"Sorry, didn't realise you hadn't seen me," Jesse grinned.

"No, no, it's fine, I was just thinking. Yes, please, come
in and do me — I mean — sort me — my wall," Mel rambled,
going red.

Jesse laughed. He had a nice laugh actually. Throaty and
loud and — shit, she was staring. She focused instead on the
hideous hairy beast on his top lip. The moustache made him
look like a seventies porn star. Urgh. That was better.

She led him back into the shop and went to retrieve her
breakfast.

"Can I get you anything?" she asked, indicating the
coffee maker.

"Nah, I'm good, but cheers," he replied, looking a little

surprised. "I'll get that heater and get started, yeah?" He wandered to the back, and Mel couldn't help notice his arse in his well-fitting jeans. She wondered what his story was, how old he was.

The bell tinkled and she turned to see her mother, dressed in an old pair of paint-splattered workman's overalls and her hair in a turban. She lugged in a large bundle wrapped in an old orange candlewick bedspread. "Melody, my love," she called, "wait till you see what I've made. It's a masterpiece, even if I do say so myself."

Mel eyed the package dubiously as Marion hefted it onto a coffee table and began carefully unwrapping it.

"I think it would look lovely with a pot plant in it," her mother said. "A maidenhair fern would be perfect." She finished the unveiling and stood back, arms wide. "Ta-da."

The 'masterpiece' turned out to be a clay sculpture about half a metre tall. From Mel's angle, the two odd lumps at the top looked a bit like someone's arse. As she circled round to look at the front, a phallic-looking protrusion, painted purple, made her choke on her toast. There was a bowl-shaped dip in the top, supposedly where the maidenhair fern would sit.

"Umm, Marion," she began, "is that—"

"It's a torso," Marion declared, "or the opposite of a bust, I suppose, whatever that's called. Isn't it fabulous?"

Mel swallowed her toast and took a sip of her coffee while she tried to think of a suitable reply. There was no way she could have that 'thing' on display in the shop.

Jesse chose that moment to come out with the heater.

"Well, hello there, gorgeous," her mother cooed, bracelets jangling as she did a little wave.

"Morning, ma'm," Jesse said, eyes widening as he walked past her art piece.

"Who is that fine hunk of a man?" Marion asked as he went through the front door.

Mel was still looking in horror at the sculpture. "What? Oh, that's Jesse," she said distractedly. "Mum, I'm sorry, but I don't think this is quite the right look for in here."

"Nonsense," her mother said firmly. "It'll look fabulous, and it'll be a wonderful talking point. I'll pop it on the shelf behind the counter, shall I?"

She sat the monstrosity next to the coffee machine, penis and blue-painted bollocks on full display, like a deformed peacock.

"Perfect," Marion declared. "I'll bring Dad in soon to see it, he'll be thrilled. Now, Melody, I must be off. Fern is having a dating scan this morning and I want to get to the farmers' market first to pick up some kale."

She pecked Mel on the cheek as she left. Jesse held open the door for her and then came in with a tool box and a piece of Gib under one arm. He looked at the sculpture behind Mel and let out another of his big laughs.

"Melody, huh?" He grinned.

Mel scowled. She wiggled the offensive sculpture around

so that its family jewels were facing the wall and sighed. She'd deal with that later.

Still, on the bright side, she could offer the bedspread to Kevin, she decided as she folded it up. She sipped her coffee. It had gone cold.

~

The day lurched from bad to worse. Ellie rang to say she had a migraine and wasn't coming in until that evening. The construction noise was driving Mel insane so she couldn't blame Ellie for wanting to avoid the place.

After a reasonably busy morning, the afternoon was quieter and she got stuck talking Shakespeare with Colin for what felt like hours. He did most of the talking. He was of the firm opinion that William was the finest writer to ever live and that nobody who came after could compare. He was very passionate about the man, and Mel found herself agreeing and unsuccessfully trying to change the subject. When Olive got up to leave, Mel was grateful for the reprieve.

"Lovely brownies, Mel," Olive said with a twinkle.

Mel laughed. "Thanks again for the recipe. I wasn't sure about the avocado but you were right, it really did make it nice and moist." She rang up Olive's book.

"Well, I have plenty more recipes if you're interested. I could email you a few ideas if you like?"

Colin huffed as they swapped email addresses and thankfully left. As she cleared cups and wiped tables, Mel thought about the possibility of a singles night for all the lonely lo-cals. Perhaps they could advertise it with a catchy name, she pondered. Something literature based maybe? She'd have a talk to Ellie about the idea.

It started to rain about three, which she hoped wouldn't put off the wine and cheese patrons for the evening. Still, the customers she had now lingered, reluctant to get wet, and so they stayed to browse the books longer or buy more coffees and she eventually ran out of brownies.

Ellie arrived at four, looking a little pale, and in flat shoes, with a shopping bag of grapes and blueberries from her local fruit and vegetable store. "The blueberries were on sale, I thought we could make muffins for tomorrow." She set the bag on the counter. "What the fuck is that?" Mel looked at where she was pointing.

"Marion," she told her by way of explanation.

"Good Lord." Ellie moved closer. "Tell me that is not a peen?"

"I wish I could," Mel sighed. "If only she'd go back to the crocheting phase. Although maybe she will, now Fern is up the duff again."

"She should do crocheted condoms. Although, I guess that horse has bolted," Ellie snorted, examining the sculp-ture more closely. "Oh lawd, it's got bloody blue balls."

They both contemplated the sculpture in silence.

"Actually, you and me both, mate," Ellie muttered. "It's been ages since I've gotten laid."

Mel had to agree. Both of them had been single for quite some time. Ellie had dumped her latest man when he decided he was serious about her and wanted to move in. She wasn't keen on cohabitation, she told Mel. Took all the fun out of it and she definitely wasn't done with her single girl lifestyle yet.

Mel had broken up with her ex when George got sick. He'd found it all a bit boring and a mood killer, as well as a drain on their social life. Still, it had been inevitable. They'd only been going out for about six months and it wasn't an epic romance. He didn't read, for one, and he was a party boy. They'd parted ways amicably enough, as was the norm for Mel. She wasn't much for one-night stands, so it had been a bit of a dry spell, and she had to admit, she was missing having sex that involved another person being in the room.

She decided she may as well do the muffins now, while it was quiet, and get an extra half hour sleep in. Or, she told herself, she could get motivated and go for a run before she opened in the morning. The Botanic Gardens would be nice.

She filled Ellie in on the repairs as they took out platters and glasses for the evening.

"I forgot to ask, how was your date with Nate?"

"Very awkward," Mel replied, "and expensive." She explained about his forgotten wallet.

"Oldest trick in the book," Ellie declared. "Though weird, he looks like he's pretty flush. Those fancy suits he wears must cost a bomb."

"I guess it could have been genuine. Maybe he really did leave his wallet behind."

"Maybe. How often do you ever do that though? It's always the first thing I check. Before even my house keys. Or my lippy. Could be an excuse to invite you on another date."

"I hope not. I don't think we've got a lot in common, to be honest."

A group of women came in, chattering and laughing, and Ellie moved away to greet them while Mel went out back to redo her lippy and hair.

They had a basic premise for their platters; they offered a variety of cheeses customers could choose. These were served with bread and good crackers and a few simple ingredients — whatever Ellie had picked up during the week — to keep things interesting. They were easy to assemble between the two of them, even if they were busy, and didn't involve a lot of wastage or kitchen space. This was good, as the kitchen was on the small side.

Ellie knew wine but slowly Mel had been learning and she was developing a pretty good palate, especially for reds.

Mel turned on the small gas fire to make the room cosy, even though it was November and not cold despite the rain. Her favourite customer came in, removing his coat and hat and hanging them on the rack.

"My dear girl. How are you? You look well."

"Albert," Mel called, going over to the old man. "It's lovely to see you."

She led Albert to a small table near the fire. He had taken to coming to the bookshop at least once a week and it was lovely he was here to support them at night.

"Can I get you a drink? Something to eat?"

"I'll have a glass of port, my dear, and a small piece of Cheddar, if you have it. Maybe some crackers and chutney to go with it, if it's not too much bother?"

"Of course it's no bother. Would you like to have a look at our menu?"

"No, no, that's fine. I haven't got time for all those fancy cheeses, just the Cheddar would be lovely." He gave her a beaming smile. "I'll choose a book while you get that, shall I? I must say, I did enjoy *The Nightingale*, thank you, it was a lovely suggestion."

"One of my regulars, Olive, recommended it to me. I'm so glad you liked it."

As she went behind the counter to get Albert his port she thought again about the singles night and mentioned it to Ellie who was getting glasses and a bottle of Pinot Gris for the group of ladies. Albert's wife Lois had died earlier in the year and he was obviously lonely. Not that Mel was planning on being matchmaker for a ninety-two-year-old man, but there must be loads of people in the community who would appreciate being able to meet potential partners, or new friends, somewhere other than a crowded Courtenay

Place bar.

It was definitely worth a try, they decided, and could become a regular thing if it was successful.

~

The evening was busier than the previous Friday had been and Mel was feeling hopeful as she and Ellie cleaned up afterwards. They hadn't sold many books but there was huge potential to hold events, she thought. Quiz nights with a literary theme, poetry slam evenings, the book club she was already planning. If the price for success was missing out on a social life, well, at least she was doing something she loved, and if they did well enough they might eventually be able to employ a part-time staff member. In any case, if her awful date with Nate was anything to go by, she wasn't missing much.

For some reason, thinking about dating made her think of Jesse. Not that she wanted to date him, of course, although maybe someone who looked like him. Firm and tanned and probably good with his hands. She thought about his hands.

Not that I'd date him, she told herself. Again. He was way too rough around the edges. Mel wasn't a snob. She wasn't. But he was ... a yob, she thought rather uncharacteristically. She needed someone who was a bit more sophisticated surely. Who dressed well, and read books and... anyway, just because he had nice hands ...

Mel decided to go to bed with a good book.

Chapter eight

"Nobody can tell what I suffer! But it is always so.
Those who do not complain are never pitied."

Pride and Prejudice, Jane Austen

Saturday had gone in a blur. Mel actually did get up and go for a run and the shop had been busy both during the day and that night.

Sunday morning she walked down to the food market on the waterfront and picked up some fruit and veges to do some juicing. She and Ellie took turns working on Sundays and Ellie was off today.

When she got back, she baked some lemonade scones and threw in a load of laundry and felt quite productive and on top of things. They opened and closed a bit later on Sundays. The weather was beautiful, so she set up their outdoor table and put up the daisy print umbrella where she sat with a glass of ginger, lemon, celery and pineapple juice. It tasted good, so she added the juice to their menu that day.

She had started to get to know a few locals, and a lot of them had kids. They were looking for someone to do a children's reading circle on Sundays to encourage parents to bring their kids and stay for a coffee and a browse.

The sun was out, she was full of hope for the future, and there was no distraction of construction or sweaty, tattooed builders to ruin her mood.

Just after two-thirty, her sister arrived with the boys. They had backpacks with them, stuffed full, and Mel knew before Fern opened her mouth what she was going to say.

"Melly, my favourite, bestest sister," she began.

"Mum says we can sleep over," Flint interrupted.

"I said if Aunty Mel didn't mind," Fern quickly put in.

"Can we? We'll be good," Blade pleaded.

Mel looked at their eager faces. She didn't have the heart to say no. She loved these boys so much. A fact Fern was counting on.

"Fine," she conceded. "But I have a yoga class at eleven tomorrow," she told Fern. "Wait, what about school?"

"Oh, I'll be back by then. We're only going to friends in the Hutt, then a quick breakfast and we'll come get them."

Mel offered her a juice but Fern screwed her nose up.

"Don't you have any soda? I can't even drink coffee at the

moment. Makes me nauseous. Man, I hate being pregnant."
She looked at her phone. "I'd better go, I want to get my nails
done for tonight. See ya, boys," she called and she was off.

Mel set Blade and Flint up at a table near the kitchen with
some colouring and a scone each. She needed them in sight.
Blade was an easy kid, quiet and industrious, and she knew
he'd help her with Flint. He was only five, but three years
ago at the same age Blade had definitely not been as full on.
Flint's concentration span was terrible and Mel suspected
he might have a bit of ADHD. Marion insisted he was merely
'high spirited' and Fern had been the same.

It was lucky the shop was quieter now. At four she turned
the closed sign, put away the outdoor table, and set about
cleaning the coffee machine.

"Shall we make pizzas for dinner?"

"Can I make mine in a rocket shape?" Flint asked.

"Sure," Mel agreed. "What about you, Blade?"

"I like them round."

"Me too. Do you want to pick some basil for me from the
pot out the back?"

"No — me," Flint insisted.

"You don't know which one's basil," Blade told him
indignantly.

"Do too," Flint wailed.

"You can help me then," Blade said and they took off to
the tiny courtyard out the back that held the shed, a clothes-
line and a few planter boxes of herbs.

Mel started on a pizza dough and while it was resting, swept and mopped the floor.

The boys came back with basil and then went upstairs to play with the box of toys Mel kept there for them.

When she was done with tidying up, she called the boys down to assemble the pizzas.

Flint's rocket looked far more like Marion's sculpture than something NASA would approve of, Mel noted, but he ate the lot, even with basil on it, when he usually objected to anything green.

Mel pulled out the old futon couch into a bed. She'd had the thing since uni days, and it was perfect for the boys. They all lay on it and ate in front of her computer, watching cartoons. She had Trumpets in the freezer that she saved for when the boys visited, and they each ate one while Sponge-Bob and Patrick set off to Shell City.

"Do you guys need to shower?"

"*No*," Flint insisted.

"We had a bath last night," Blade told her. Mel mulled it over and figured it wouldn't hurt to miss one night, so she let it go.

"Tooth-brushing time then."

"I forgot my toothbrush," Flint told her.

"You did not," Blade said.

"Did too."

"I saw it in your bag," his brother said. Flint dissolved into tears. It was seven-thirty and Mel guessed he was tired.

"How about we just do a finger brush?" she suggested. She suspected his brush was there, but figured it was an aunt's right to skip on the boring parenting stuff sometimes.

Flint insisted on a book, but only made it five pages into *The Gruffalo* before he was asleep. He was adorable asleep, she thought, brushing back his blond curls.

The boys were like chalk and cheese. Flint, a mini Fern. Pale, blond and blue eyed. The only thing like his father were his freckles. Blade was very much like his dad — dark skinned, brown eyed and solid.

Blade was an avid reader, and he really into Captain Underpants at the moment, so Mel let him read for half an hour before telling him it was time to put the book down. It was only just after eight, but because the apartment was so small, she didn't like to disturb Blade by leaving the light on to read while he was trying to sleep, so she showered quickly and put on her oldest and most comfy pair of pyjamas and hopped into bed, leaving the door cracked open in case the boys needed her in the night.

The old building creaked and groaned. There was still street noise outside. She lay thinking about what needed doing for the next week and listened to the quiet snuffling of the boys. The occasional voice drifted up from the street. A dog barked in the distance. Mel's eyes drifted shut.

She dreamt she was wading through a river where a large purple dinosaur, smoking a pipe, was chasing her, demanding she give him her socks.

She was woken early by a small torpedo. Flint leapt on the bed beside her insisting they have pancakes.

"Come onnnn, Aunty Mel, I'm starving!" he shouted in her ear. "A man's gotta eat," he told her solemnly. Mel laughed.

"You're not a man," Blade told him.

"Am too."

"Okay, okay." Mel got up and clapped her hands, ready to avert another argument.

She pulled on her dressing gown and shuffled into her slippers.

"Who wants lemon and who wants syrup?"

After a large pancake breakfast, Mel got the boys dressed and ready for school. Flint was complaining of a sudden sore stomach and saying he was too sick to go. He'd eaten three pancakes at his insistence and in spite of Mel's objections. Fern lived in Johnsonville, which was a good twenty-minute drive away, and it was already eight-thirty but there was no sign of the boys' mother, and she wasn't answering her phone. Neither was Marion, although that wasn't unusual. Her parents refused to own a mobile and the house phone was often ignored if they were working.

Mel didn't have a car, and it was too far for the boys to walk to school.

Just as she started booking an Uber, Flint threw up, all over the futon and himself.

Shit.

"Blade, honey, can you find me a number for your school?" she asked him, handing him her phone.

She took Flint into the bathroom and stripped him off, turning on the shower to heat up.

"Wait here," she told him, and went to strip the boys' sheets.

Blade handed her back the phone and she hit dial. After she left an absentee message on the answer machine, she left another for Fern and then she wrangled a screaming Flint into the shower. He needed a hair wash, which he considered torture, and by the time they were done, she was soaked and they were both exhausted.

She put him into her bed with more cartoons and an empty ice-cream container, and set Blade up downstairs where he started on his school reading without any fuss. She gave the top of his head a kiss as she went back up to sort the laundry. Flint was fast asleep.

After a quick shower herself and a disinfection of the bathroom just in case, Mel went down and did a shopping list for the week's baking and platters. She helped Blade with some maths and tried Fern again. It was after ten, but there was still no answer.

She texted her friend Laura to say she wouldn't make yoga, and then she cleaned the downstairs bathroom and topped up the paper towels and hand soap. She thought about calling Nate to check up on the railing but decided she couldn't deal with him today.

The blade saw started up next door. There was a loud crash and swearing and she heard Jesse's dog barking on the back of the ute.

Fern arrived at quarter past eleven, breezing in with a couple of shopping bags and a takeaway coffee cup in her hand.

Mel counted to ten in her head. Then she did it again. She sent Blade upstairs to get their bags.

"Where have you been?" she asked. Her tone came out slightly more bitchy than she was trying for.

"Oh, I slept in. We stayed so late last night and I was knackered. You don't know what it's like carrying another person around all the time, Mel, it's exhausting."

Mel was about to reply when Blade came running downstairs. "Aunty Mel, Flint's gone."

Chapter nine

*"How clever you are, to know something
of which you are ignorant."*

Pride and Prejudice, Jane Austen

General chaos ensued. Mel and Blade searched the apartment, the bookstore and the back courtyard. There was no sign of him. Fern sat and wailed at the table and repeated "Where is he? Where is he?" over and over until Mel wanted to slap her. Blade started to cry. Mel felt sick. "It's okay," she told him, trying to sound calm, "we'll find him." She turned to Fern. "Should we call the police?"

Fern wailed louder and then there was a bang on the front door, before it swung open and Jesse was there, a pissed-off expression on his face and a wriggling child tucked under one muscled arm.

"I'm not running a bloo—", he looked at Blade, "blimmin'

daycare next door," he told Mel as he set Flint down inside. "It's a building site. My building site. Where my — bum's — on the line if OSH finds small kids and half-naked women with no hard hats wandering around whenever they blim-min' well want."

Flint ran to his mother, grinning widely, looking uncon-cerned and a little pleased with himself.

"He's got a doggy," he told the room, "and I patted-ed it and it licked my face all over," he announced proudly.

Blade had stopped crying and was half hidden behind Mel, looking nervously at Jesse.

Mel gave him a gentle squeeze to reassure him.

"Thank you so much for bringing him back." Fern had leapt to her feet, and was holding out a hand to Jesse. "I don't think we've met, I'm Fern, Mel's sister. The boys were staying with her, and I had no idea she would let them run off unsupervised like that."

Mel stared at her sister as she shook Jesse's hand. Sure, she was technically at fault, she supposed, since the boys were in her care, but she was also a little angry right now. She knelt down and took Flint's hand.

"Flinny, sweet, look at Aunty Mel, okay." She waited for him to look at her before she continued, trying to keep her voice level. "That was very, very naughty. You know you don't go outside without asking me first. You can't leave and not tell me. It's not okay. And you don't pat strange dogs. Ever. It could have bitten you. I'm very cross with you right now, and you can't come and stay with me if you don't follow the rules."

Flint burst into loud sobbing tears.

"Mel," said Fern crossly, "now look what you've done. You've upset him." She opened up her arms for Flint and cuddled him.

"It's all right, baby, Aunty Melly's being a big meany, isn't she."

Mel could feel her blood pressure rising. She stood back up and glared at Fern. "He needs to learn—" she started but Fern cut her off. "Come on, boys, let's go and leave Mel to her work," she said snarkily, with an irritating emphasis on 'work'.

She shuffled a still-crying Flint out the door. Blade trailed behind them, looking back at Mel.

"Bye," he said sadly. "Thank you for having us."

Mel blew him a kiss. "Love you, buddy. I'll see you soon, okay?"

He gave her a small smile that faded as he looked at Jesse, then he left, forlornly dragging both backpacks behind him.

Mel regarded Jesse, who was still standing there, looking stony faced. She sighed.

"Look, I'm sorry. I didn't know he'd gotten out," she started. "It won't happen again."

"Well, it better bloody not," he told her. "Building sites are dangerous. And kids need twenty-four/seven supervision. You can't just parent them when it suits, while you swan around drinking wine and reading books."

Mel had had enough.

"Look, you complete dickhead, I said sorry. I know I fucked up, okay?" She was shouting now, and she was struggling not to cry. Partly because she was so relieved Flint was okay, and partly because she cried when she was angry. "There's no need to harp on. I get it. Now just PISS OFF."

It was spoiled a little by the hitch in her voice as she said it, and the fact that she felt like a bitch the minute it came out her mouth.

She looked at Jesse, opened her mouth to apologise and then saw his face. He looked fed up and wary. He turned and left, closing the door with a quiet snick that was more telling than if he'd slammed it behind him.

She burst into tears.

That afternoon, as she brought in the sheets from the line, she thought about going over and apologising to Jesse. He had a point. It was her fault. She should have checked Flint more. Maybe she should take over some muffins to say sorry. But when she went back inside she saw his ute pulling out. As he drove past, he saw her. She raised her hand to wave but he beat her to it, pointedly raising his middle finger straight up at her.

"Up yours, Jesse!" she yelled to the empty street.

Chapter ten

"This is too much, to remember at night all the foolish things that were said in the morning."

Pride and Prejudice, Jane Austen

Mel tossed and turned all night and woke with a headache and feeling a bit sick. She worried that she might have picked up Flint's bug but when she rang to find out how he was doing, he was fine and back at school. Fern then rambled on about her pregnancy and how she was 'at that exhausting stage' and that she was convinced this one would be a girl.

"I've been thinking about names. What do you think about Amber? Or maybe Jade?"

"What does Chase think?"

"Chase? He'll go along with whatever I choose. He's not the one that has to carry the bloody thing for nine months. Well, I guess only five months now, since I didn't realise."

Less time for her to complain, Mel thought, but kept quiet.

"What are you thinking for a boy?" she asked instead.

"It's not going to be a boy. I really want a little girl that I can dress up and do girly things with," Fern replied airily.

~

The morning was quiet. Olive had come in and told Mel about a new business tax break she hadn't realised she was eligible for. She also told Mel about a new author she'd read a review for and asked Mel to order the book for her.

Olive was sitting with her pot of Earl Grey in her spot by the window by the time Ellie arrived, late again, and Mel was feeling better. That was, until the door opened with a flourish and Colin came in, a stack of papers tucked under his arm.

"Ahh, there you are." He smiled at her, his small mouth pursed like a lizard. Where else he thought she'd be, on a Tuesday morning during opening hours, she had no idea.

"I was hoping you'd do me the favour of putting one of these in your window. I'm sure it's right up your alley in any case."

He handed Mel a piece of paper and she glanced at it. It was a flyer for an upcoming Shakespeare weekend in Christchurch next January.

"Of course, Colin, no problem at all."

Colin fiddled with the stack of remaining papers, straightening them neatly together.

"Actually, I had rather hoped you might accompany me to Christchurch for the weekend. I'm sure we would have a jolly good time as we do seem to have a lot in common. There will be readings, performances, and I thought we could sign up for the Midsummer Night Writing Workshop." He chuckled at the pun.

Mel tried not to look horrified at the thought.

"I'm so sorry, Colin, but I absolutely won't be able to spare the time off," she said firmly. "Not with a new business to run, it would be irresponsible of me to shirk my duties, I'm afraid."

Colin looked crestfallen. Mel heard Ellie do an amused little cough from where she was huddled over the accounts in the back room and just prayed she wasn't going to say anything to add to the awkwardness of the situation. Or, God forbid, tell her she'd man the shop.

"Well, that is a shame. Still, if you change your mind ..."

"I'll put this up in the window now. I'm sure plenty of our customers will be interested."

"I'll leave you a few spare copies, so you can hand them out to interested parties."

Colin gave her the entire pile of remaining flyers, did a weird little bow and thankfully left straight away.

After Mel had taped the notice to the corner of the front window, she came back to find Olive standing at the counter, a Nora Roberts book clutched to her bosom.

"I'll take this one today, thank you, Mel, and would I be

able to have one of those Shakespeare pamphlets? I do adore Shakespeare, not that I'd be brave enough to go along to something like that, without knowing anyone there."

"Of course you could," Mel told her kindly as she rang up the book. "I'm sure you'd meet some wonderful people, and there'd bound to be other people there by themselves."

"I'm not sure I'm clever enough for a gathering of Shakespeare aficionados."

"You're a very smart lady, Olive. You certainly know more about Shakespeare than I do."

Olive flushed at the compliment. She took a flyer from Mel and folded it carefully, tucking it into the pocket of her voluminous brown cardigan.

~

The rest of the week passed fairly quickly and they were surprisingly busy. It was heartening how the local community supported new businesses and they had plenty of new customers popping in to check them out, both during the day and at night, as well as many returnees, which was nice to see. Ellie commented that she thought it was going better than she'd expected, as she restocked the bar for Friday night.

Ellie had worked front of house in bars during uni and had also worked in her parents' vineyard doing wine tours before they'd started the business, and Mel was happy to leave the picking of wines to her friend. She liked what she liked, she'd told Ellie, but she didn't have a clue what was good. Ellie was gradually educating her — which was really an excuse for cracking open a bottle and having a glass every now and then.

"We really need to have a night out sometime," Ellie sighed as she sipped her Pinot Gris. "It's been ages. Not since before we started doing the renovations."

"I know. We're turning into crusty old spinsters."

"Two-for-one cocktails on a Tuesday? Shit, does anyone even go out on a Tuesday?"

"Mainly people turning eighteen or fifty and couples celebrating an anniversary," Mel replied gloomily. "How depressing. Next week then?"

They lifted their glasses and clinked them together to seal the deal. Mel nibbled on a rather good piece of smoked Gouda. This was probably all they'd get to eat before the evening rush started.

"I've got a student coming in to see me tomorrow. She's keen to do the children's sessions on Sundays. If things keep going well, perhaps she could help out in the evenings every now and then to give us a night off."

"Problem is," Ellie said around a mouthful of bread, "that you're the only person I go out with these days. Aside from Geri, I hardly see anyone else and she's away working more often than not."

Geri worked as a marketing manager for a cosmetic company and spent most of her time at meetings in Auckland or travelling to Australia. She was the ideal flatmate — pleasant when she was there and offering a steady supply of free makeup samples.

"I guess it would be nice to be able to go on a date sometime when it wasn't a school night though."

"You got any prospective suitors in mind then?"

"No," Ellie said looking depressed. "I was thinking I might have to try to lure that sexy Colin away from you."

"You're welcome to him."

"I think I'd have a more interesting evening with Albert, to be honest."

Mel couldn't argue with that.

On Saturday morning Mel almost fell down the stairs as the banister swayed and teetered in her hand.

"Shit." She pulled her phone out of her running jacket to text Nate to remind him about having it fixed.

By the time she'd got back from her jog, there was still no reply.

She was feeling positive though as she got into the shower. The gardens had been beautiful to run through in the spring sunshine and she'd be able to put the outside table and umbrella up again today. Going downstairs to make iced tea to serve, she thought of all the books she'd read over the years that were set in the Southern States of America where they'd sit on porches drinking tinkling glasses of the long, cool drink. She was putting two jugs into the fridge to chill, when her phone dinged.

It was Nate.

Sure gorgeous, gettin on 2 that nxt wk. How bout drinks 2nite? My house?

She texted back:

Sorry, working as usual. Let me know about the stairs.

~

The student, Sophie, turned out to be perfect for their children's sessions. She agreed to start the following Sunday as a trial and they discussed children's books and a vague programme. Sophie had a lot of ideas, which was great. She was studying to be a play specialist and the hours suited her perfectly.

"It must be so nice, owning a bookshop," Sophie sighed, glancing at a display Mel had been working on earlier. "All these books, begging to be read. I'd probably never get anything done. Not that I'll let that distract me," she added quickly.

"You'd think so, wouldn't you?" Mel replied. "The irony is though that I don't get nearly as much time as I'd like to read these days."

They discussed their favourite books for a while before Sophie left. Mel vowed to make more time for reading and plucked a book she'd been eyeing off the shelf, settling behind the counter with it.

~

The shop had become busy in the afternoon and by the time Ellie arrived at four for the evening, Mel had already served three groups of afternoon customers with cheese and wine. Two couples lingered, sipping a second bottle of wine and talking books together, lounging happily, a half-eaten platter on the table between them. Ellie grinned at Mel when she saw them; this was exactly what they'd imagined when they'd first talked about opening the shop.

While Ellie took over downstairs, Mel went upstairs for a cup of tea and a bit of a break. The weather was becoming warmer and she felt sticky and hot and needed a shower. As she tidied up and removed a stray shoe from under the sofa she smiled to herself; one of Flint's pictures had somehow slipped under the bed unseen. It was of a boy with a scribble of yellow hair, who she took to be Flint, handing a bunch of purple and green flowers to a woman with long brown hair and what looked like some kind of patterned trousers, who she gathered was her.

Thinking of Flint made her think fleetingly of Jesse. She hadn't seen him since Monday, thankfully, but now she felt indignation and fury bubble up inside her. He was such a dick. Even if he had been technically right, he still didn't need to be such an arsehole to her. She pushed any thought of him aside, and went over to her little kitchenette where she flicked on the kettle, reaching into the cupboard for a box of soothing camomile tea.

Chapter eleven

"Follies and nonsense, whims and inconsistencies, do divert me, I own, and I laugh at them whenever I can."

Pride and Prejudice, Jane Austen

They had gotten so busy later that Mel didn't notice Nate had come in until he leant over and kissed her on the cheek. He smelt like expensive aftershave.

"Nate," she squawked. "What are you doing here?"

"Well, I thought as the landlord I'd better come and see what you get up to here in the evenings. And, like they say, 'If you can't bring the mountain to Mohammed ...' You're always too busy working to go out with me."

Ellie, saint that she was, appeared right then as if by magic to show Nate to a table.

"I'd prefer to sit in the back," he said.

"He has good taste in wine, I'll give him that," Ellie mentioned a few minutes later as she poured a glass of one of the most expensive wines they served. "It's probably a good thing we're serving the truffle oil this week."

"Not that we need to impress him," Mel said.

"He is pretty nice looking though, you have to admit."

"You seem to think everyone's attractive at the moment. I really think you need a shag."

"Tuesday," Ellie said with a wink. "Ooh, we should get dumplings first."

"Okay, but I'm not too sure what dumplings have to do with sex."

"Nothing, I just like dumplings," Ellie laughed. "But now who's thinking of sex?"

Mel glanced over at Nate but found he was looking at her so she quickly looked away and hurried over to fill another table's water glasses. He was good looking, that was true, but there was something about him that she couldn't quite put her finger on. Perhaps he was a little too polished for her? Jesse, on the other hand, was too unpolished. There was no winner here. She also needed to stop thinking about Jesse at random times of the day and night.

She couldn't avoid Nate entirely though so eventually had to approach him and ask if he'd like another glass of wine.

"No chance of you joining me?"

"Afraid not. It looks like we're going to be busy for a good few hours yet."

This was probably not entirely true but Mel was worried she'd encourage him if she said otherwise.

"I'd best be off when I've finished this glass anyway." Nate glanced at his watch. He wasn't in a suit tonight, but a pair of tailored black trousers and a pale-blue shirt with yellow and white polka dot cuffs. Bespoke, she guessed.

Mel was distracted by a table needing service so she didn't see him get up and leave, but when she looked around short-ly after, he was gone.

"Ellie, did Nate pay his bill?" she asked, as Ellie passed her a few minutes later.

"Not to me he didn't, but I was out the back putting the empties in the dumpster and he was having a blazing row in the street with Claire. Then she disappeared up her back stairs and he followed her."

"Strange. Do you think he owns her building too?"

"I've no idea, but she was angry about something."

"Well, he didn't pay when he left. Just because he owns the bloody building doesn't mean he gets a free ride. And good luck to her if she's trying to get him to fix something."

Ellie was working in the shop on Sunday and Mel had come downstairs to nab some leftovers from the night before for her lunch when Claire breezed through the door. She was about to slink back upstairs but remembered what Ellie had said about seeing her with Nate the night before. She was curious.

"Hi, Claire, have you come over for a glass of wine?" Ellie

asked cheerfully.

Claire sniffed. "Most definitely not, quite the opposite in fact."

"Oh?"

"I wanted to make sure you do in fact have a liquor licence to be operating these premises as a wine bar at night. I found a cigarette butt right in my front entrance this morning."

"We do indeed," Ellie told her, indicating their licence which was proudly displayed behind the bar. Right next to Marion's ugly torso art piece, which was still facing the wall, turning the other cheek, so to speak.

Claire's eyes widened in horror. "I do wonder whether you would have been better to set up right in the city," she said. "We're aiming for more of a village feel here."

"Ah, like France?" Ellie asked brightly.

"Exactly."

"Funny, we have two French wines on our menu at the moment. In fact, one of them I had in a tiny wine bar when I was in a village in Bordeaux last year." Ellie gave her a wide smile, rather like a crocodile might to a chicken. If she'd been aiming for innocent, Mel felt like she failed miserably.

"Not that we're a wine bar, exactly," Mel added. "We're still a bookshop. You should come over one evening, Claire. We'd love to give you a complimentary glass, as a fellow villager."

"I don't drink," Claire retorted tightly, "and I do think there is a huge difference between property-owning residents such as myself and fly-by-nighters like the two of you who waft in and disturb the peace and are gone as soon as their business hits difficult times." She turned on her heel. "I've seen your type before."

Mel was speechless as Claire headed out the door.

"Nasty, sanctimonious cow," Ellie muttered.

"Nasty, sanctimonious, property-owning cow," Mel corrected. "But if she owns her building, what was Nate doing there last night?"

~

Mel found as she shut the shop at five on Tuesday she was looking forward to going out that night. It had been a while since she and Ellie had cut loose. Not that there would be much happening in the city on a Tuesday, but she'd be happy with some nice food, a few cocktails and the chance to hang out with Ellie away from the shop for a change. After making an apple cake for the next day, she went upstairs and showered and contemplated her wardrobe. It would be nice to dress up a bit and make an effort, she decided, so she pulled out a short, fitted black skirt she hadn't worn in over a year and a sheer white blouse that was just the right side of see-through.

Ellie was looking stunning, as usual, when she turned up an hour later. She was wearing the emerald blouse she'd bought a couple of weeks earlier with several of the buttons undone and her hot-pink bra was visible every time she leant forward. If Mel's skirt was fitted, Ellie's looked like it was painted on, barely skimming the tops of her thighs. Her signature heels gave her the extra inches she was always craving.

"Look at us, all dressed up for a Tuesday night." She kissed Mel on the cheek.

~

They decided to walk down to a local first, the Thistle Inn. The building was historic, a large, white square building that was one of Wellington's oldest. It had featured in one of Katherine Mansfield's short stories, and was steeped in history. They also did a mean deep-fried pickle.

While they ate, and drank a cocktail, they talked about ideas for their first Christmas in the store.

"We'll need to decorate, of course," Mel said, "but we need to either do it cheap and cheerful, or invest in some pieces we can use for years to come."

"I'm thinking a fairly plain tree, maybe red bows, and a dove on top, with plain paper packages tied in string underneath," Ellie said. "Old-fashioned style."

"Yes, I like it," Mel enthused. "Maybe I'll do Christmas mince pies and truffles on the platters? I could do candy cane hot chocolates."

"We should probably look for some good-priced bubbles too."

"Ooh, should we do a little testing tonight?" Mel suggested, wiggling her eyebrows.

"Hmmm, maybe," Ellie said carefully, "but we always end up drunk as skunks on bubbles."

They sat and grinned at each for a bit and Ellie stood up. "Glass or whole bottle then?" she asked.

~

After they polished off their bubbles, they wandered down to the waterfront.

They popped into the Foxglove and had another bubbly test taste. It was pretty quiet there, so eventually they wandered along looking for someplace that had more of a crowd.

Mac's had good music playing and the tables out the front were almost full. They decided to go in and check it out, and also use the loo.

It was loud and hot inside. There was a group of suits at one end of the room, drinking wine and chatting loudly over the music. The bar was busy as well with only two staff on, so Mel offered to get drinks while Ellie went to the ladies.

"Bubbles or a cocktail?" she asked.

"Surprise me." Ellie toddled off. She was impressive at walking in heels, even when drunk, Mel thought. She was glad she had height and didn't need to wear anything much more than a wedge.

She pushed through a group of guys towards the bar and had ordered two Rosebuds when someone behind her called out, "Hey, it's the book chick."

When she turned, the lanky young guy from Jesse's crew

was grinning broadly at her. Mel couldn't remember his name, or even whether they'd been introduced.

"Hey," she said.

"Come and join us," the kid invited, gesturing down the bar. Mel guessed 'us' might include Jesse, and, sure enough, there he was, casually leaning against a high table, laughing with one of the guys from the site. He was all smiles, and wearing a cute black, short-sleeved shirt with the cuffs rolled. It had pink flamingos all over it. She had to admit, he looked good. Apart from the moustache, she reminded herself.

"Um, I'm waiting on a friend," she said vaguely, hoping that would deter him, but then Ellie popped up beside her and took one of the drinks from the bar.

"Ohh, yum, Rosebuds." She took a sip. "Hello, cutie," she directed at the apprentice.

The guy's eyes roamed over Ellie like a starving man in the desert. He did a cute little head tilt and blushed a little as he gave Ellie a shy smile.

"Wow. Hi." The smile grew into a grin. "Man, you are *hot*," he declared.

"Ha, cute," Ellie laughed.

"I'm Aaron," he told her.

"Ellie," she replied.

"These are the guys who are working on the art gallery next door to the shop," Mel said.

"Want to come join us?" he asked, hopefully, pointing at

their group again.

"Sure," Ellie agreed, and Mel did a little internal sigh. She didn't want to talk to Jesse, so she made sure to stand as far away from him as possible when they got to the table.

Aaron did the introductions.

"So this is Len," he told them, pointing to an older guy with a weathered face and a goatee. He gave them a nod. "Ladies," he said cheerfully.

"And that's Hoppy," Aaron continued, waving at a big guy with a beer gut who was talking to Mark, the plumber. "And Mark, and our boss Pete," Aaron said, going round the group in turn. "Jesse, the foreman — we're in construction," he told Ellie a bit shyly. "Jono, he's a sparkie, and Griff, his mate," he finished.

There was a general murmur of hellos from the guys.

"This is Ellie," Aaron said, looking longingly at her. "And, umm, the bookstore chick. Sorry, I don't know your name?"

"Mel." She took another sip of her drink. "Ellie and I are business partners." Don't look at him, she told herself, trying to ignore Jesse. She made a point of looking across at the guy next to her and smiling.

"So, Griff," she said politely, "what is it you do?"

"I'm a personal trainer," he told her. "At Buffs Gym, up the top of Thorndon Quay."

He did have a very nice body, Mel thought, toned and lean and a nice, smiling face. They talked a bit about yoga, and running and keto diets before Ellie interrupted them.

"Mel, Aaron's said he'd get us more drinks, what do you want?"

"Aaron?" said Hoppy with a booming laugh. "Skiddy, you mean."

The guys all laughed and Aaron went red.

"It's just a nickname and not for what you think."

"Okay, this I gotta hear," Ellie laughed.

Mark offered to get the next round instead and Mel and Ellie asked for a vodka tonic each. It seemed a bit rude to order expensive cocktails.

'Skiddy' told them about how on his first day on the job, he'd turned up in his mum's Suzuki Swift, and as he pulled up, braked a little too vigorously, doing a huge skid on the gravel drive, in front of the whole crew, spraying them with grit.

"I'd only got my licence the week before," he said to explain it. "So you see, it's nothing to do with toilets or anything." He blushed again as he looked at Ellie. He reminded Mel of a cute puppy.

"Jesus, how old are you anyway?" Ellie asked with a grin.

"I'll be twenty next week, on Monday," he told her.

"Lord, that makes me feel old," she moaned theatrically. "I'm almost ten years older than you."

"Oh, but you look amazing," Skiddy said earnestly. "I love older women."

Ellie laughed awkwardly.

"Just not older than ya mum, right, Skids?" Jono put in.

"There's a 'your mum' joke in there somewhere," Len laughed.

Mark came back with the drinks and they all carefully extracted them from his grip. Jesse had remained fairly quiet, Mel thought, as she snuck a look at him. He had his bottle tilted up, and his Adam's apple was moving as he gulped down a good chug of beer. He had beautiful skin and the leather cord of a necklace he wore dipped down into his shirt where Mel could see the top of another tattoo. She looked back at Griff who smiled at her.

"So anyway, if you want to come check out the gym, let me know," he said, as though their earlier conversation hadn't been interrupted.

She smiled. "Thanks, but I don't think I'm a gym person. I get bored."

"Well, you look like a gym person," Griff told her. "You have great calves."

"Oh, well, thanks," Mel blushed. "That could be the yoga, I guess."

Jesse leant over the bar and caught her eye.

"Hey, bookworm, where's ya man tonight?"

Mel looked at him in surprise. Was he trying to cockblock her? And the way he'd said 'bookworm' wasn't cute. It implied she was a nerdy little grub.

"For your information," she said primly, "I'm single. I don't have a boyfriend. Caterpillar lip," she added snootily.

Griff and Mark both laughed.

"It's for Movember," Jesse said indignantly.

Chapter twelve

*"Their eyes instantly met, and the cheeks of both
were overspread with the deepest blush."*

Pride and Prejudice, Jane Austen

Mel and Ellie got steadily drunker with the guys. She was actually having a great time. Pete had gone home about nine, claiming the wife would kill him if he came home loaded on a Tuesday again. They'd all been out to celebrate a new contract they had won for a restoration project starting in the new year.

Once he'd gone, the guys all relaxed a bit. They obviously felt more at ease without the boss there.

Mel asked Skiddy how long he'd been apprenticing for.

"Coming up three years," he told her. "I left school at the end of year twelve and went straight into it. I was lucky 'cause my brother is a mate of Jesse's."

Jesse looked up at the mention of his name.

"Doesn't mean you get any favours though," he said. " Although I think we went pretty easy on you with the initiation stuff."

Len and Hoppy laughed at the look on Skiddy's face.

"They didn't," he insisted. "They did all sorts of shit to me."

This led to a good half hour of apprentice stories.

Hoppy told them about how he'd been sent to the store for a long weight. Len said his was a left-handed screwdriver. He'd been to four stores before he caught on, he told them.

Skiddy said he'd been locked in the portaloo for an hour after Jesse backed his ute up to the door. And that they'd changed all the names in his phone to read 'Pete' so he didn't know who was who.

"What about you, Jesse?" Ellie asked.

"I got conned into a weightlifting competition with a forty-kilogram bag of cement," he told her. "They let me get to nine lifts before they slit the bag over my head." They all laughed, including Mel, but she found herself imagining Jesse covered in sweat and concrete, and having to take off his shirt, and, bloody hell, she was horny.

He caught her staring and gave her a long look. She took another gulp of her drink and looked away.

"Wait a minute," Skiddy said suddenly. "There's no such thing as tartan paint, is there?"

Everyone cracked up. "You're adorable," Ellie told him,

then hiccuped loudly.

He gave her a big grin. "So are you," he said, gazing at her longingly.

By eleven, Mel was feeling a bit tipsy. Hoppy and Len had left, and Mark was busy chatting up the bartender. Griff had wandered off to talk to a couple of girls he seemed to vaguely know and they looked much more likely to be the gym-going type than Mel. They all got up and wandered outside.

Ellie declared she was Ubering home and Skiddy asked if he could share. Mel and Ellie hugged and did the drunk 'I love you'.

"Well," Mel said a little awkwardly to Jesse, "see you around."

They both set off walking in the same direction, but it would have been strange to have walked separately. A not-comfortable silence settled over them.

"I left my ute at the site," Jesse told her.

"Ah, right."

They carried on walking, again in silence for a bit.

"Look, I'm sorry," Mel blurted, "I've been a bit of a bitch to you, and I'm not normally like that."

Jesse glanced over at her. "Yeah, me too. I'm sorry I was a dick. I can be a bit anal about health and safety stuff. Since I became foreman, the guys tell me I've been a bit over the top with it."

They grinned at each other.

"So, truce?" he suggested.

"Truce."

They kept walking, now in a more amiable silence. Jesse had very long legs, Mel noted. Firm, muscly thighs in his black jeans.

"You seem quite young to be a foreman," she said. "How old are you anyway?"

"I have a youthful face — I'm twenty-six," he told her. "I've only been foreman since the end of last year. Pete wanted to get into the office more, now he's in his sixties."

They talked about his job as they walked up the hill. He'd left school at sixteen and started work in Hawke's Bay, but moved to Wellington a couple of years after his apprenticeship finished and began working for Pete.

When they got to the bookstore, Jesse indicated his ute still parked outside the building site.

"Well, see you around." He fished his keys out of his pocket.

"Wait, you're not driving now, are you?"

"Nah, I'll probably sleep in the car."

Mel looked at the tiny cab.

"I do have a futon," she told him slowly. "You're welcome to stay at mine."

He looked at her, his face unreadable.

"Are you sure?"

Mel felt weirdly flustered. "Yeah, it's fine. No problem."

She unlocked the front door. They walked silently through the store and went up the stairs to her apartment.

"Jesus, this railing is buggered," he told her. "You should get that sorted. It's dangerous."

"I know," Mel sighed. "I've been trying to get the landlord to sort it."

They stood awkwardly in the living room area.

Although Mel and Ellie had put a lot of effort into the downstairs, they hadn't done much to the flat above. It had unfinished walls, and visible wiring. The floors hadn't been sanded back and the fixtures were all old. The bathroom still had speckled panelling from the sixties and a peach porcelain sink. But it was clean at least.

"Bathroom is through there," she pointed a little unnecessarily, since the bedroom door was open and there was only one other door.

"Cheers."

Mel eyed the futon dubiously. It didn't seem big enough. Should she give him her bed?

Jesse came out of the bathroom. He'd taken off his shirt. The reality of him was better than her imagination. His body was amazing — muscled brown skin, with a sprinkle of chest hair and a large mandala tattoo over his left pec. Mel swallowed.

"Do you need a T-shirt?" she blurted out.

Jesse gave her a funny look. "What for?"

"Umm, to sleep in?"

"Babe, I don't think your T-shirts would fit me. And I don't normally wear a T-shirt to bed." He looked at her. "Did you want me to?"

"No," Mel said, probably too quickly. "No, no, it's fine. Really fine."

She was ridiculously turned on, she realised. It really had been a while. All this from a flash of naked chest.

"So, umm," Jesse pointed to the futon. "Do you have any blankets or ..." he trailed off.

They were both staring at each other, and it was like Mel's brain had short circuited. 'Kiss him, just kiss him', her libido was chanting. 'Kiss him.'

And then he was kissing her.

And holy hell.

Chapter thirteen

"She endeavoured to forget what she could not overlook."

Pride and Prejudice, Jane Austen

Mel cracked an eye open the next morning and groaned. What was she thinking, going out on a Tuesday and getting hammered? Experimentally she rolled over to see whether her head would tolerate the movement and found herself staring at a smooth, brown back.

Jesse must have woken then as well and sat up with a start.

He looked over to Mel and they eyed each other warily for a brief second. He was looking rather rumpled and, she was pleased to note, as though he was as hungover as she felt.

"Shit. What time is it?"

Without waiting for a reply, he leapt out of bed and pulled on his jeans, not bothering to put his underpants on. She got a brief glimpse of his arse before it disappeared into the denim.

"Fuck," he exclaimed, not looking at Mel, but retrieving his phone and checking it. He plucked his shirt from the floor, flinging it on without buttoning it. It seemed to Mel he was in a mad rush to get away from her and she felt a bit rejected.

"This was a huge mistake," she blurted into the silence. "I don't know what I was thinking, it's not something I'd normally do, if I was sober—"

Jesse scowled at her and paused while he pulled his shoes on. "What are you trying to say?" he spat out. "Do you think I jumped you because you were drunk or something? It was you who threw yourself at me first."

"I did not *throw* myself at you," Mel replied indignantly. "You were the one who kissed me."

"That's not how I remember it," Jesse smirked. "All the eye fucking?"

"You're not even my type. Especially with that ugly bloody moustache."

"Well, you're not looking so hot yourself this morning."

"Dickhead," she muttered, getting up for a glass of much-needed water, taking the sheet with her, wrapped around her body.

He'd finished putting his shoes on and with his shirt still unbuttoned moved towards the stairs.

"Thanks, I guess," he said without so much as a backward glance.

As he thundered down the stairs, Mel heard him call up, "And get these bloody stairs fixed."

"Tell my bloody landlord. I've been trying for weeks!" she hollered back.

She went back into the bedroom, flopped onto her bed and pulled the pillow over her face. What a disaster.

~

After two cups of coffee and a couple of paracetamol, Mel's head and her mood in general hadn't improved. She showered and dressed and went down to open the shop, praying she wouldn't see Colin or Claire that morning. She really didn't think she could stomach either of them and was wondering how she'd get through until closing that night.

As she glanced over at Claire's shop, she noticed Nate leaving and quickly jumped back into the doorway hoping he hadn't seen her. Watching from her shadowy spot, she saw him flick the lock on a silver Audi, get in and smoothly pull away from the curb.

What was he doing at Claire's anyway at — she checked the time on her phone — nine in the morning? Probably not buying women's clothing and, in any case, Claire didn't open until ten.

She tried to remember whether the car had been there the night before when she'd stumbled home but, to be honest, not only was she drunk but she had been quite distracted by Jesse at that point. She wasn't going to think about that now.

It had been a mistake. He obviously thought so too.

Their truce hadn't lasted long. Clearly they weren't destined to be friends. Mel only hoped they would finish the job at the art gallery soon and move on. She pushed aside thoughts of how his firm abs had felt under her hands and went into the kitchen to slice the apple cake and mix up a batch of savoury muffins.

~

The one time she would have liked a quiet shop, it wasn't. She'd sent a text to Ellie asking how she was feeling that morning and had received a message back around eleven: Crap!

Followed a few minutes later by:
Will come in early so u can have a break. Yr probs feeling like shite 2

~

As she tried to surreptitiously eat a savoury muffin for lunch during a lull, she noticed someone lurking in the classic novel section. A second glance showed that it was Skiddy. He seemed to be looking around as though searching for some assistance.

"Skiddy, can I help you with something?" He jumped at the sound of her voice.

"Er — um — just doing a bit of Christmas shopping." He quickly picked up the book that was directly in front of him.

It was *The Age of Innocence*, she noticed with some amusement. "Is — um — is Ellie in today?"

"Not yet, she's usually in about three-ish."

Skiddy's face dropped as though his favourite teddy had lost an eye.

"She might be a bit earlier today though."

He put the book back on the shelf.

"I'm not sure about this one. I might have to come and have another look around later."

Mel laughed to herself as he slunk to the door and out into the street. It was obvious he was smitten with her gorgeous friend. He wasn't the first and wouldn't be the last.

Ellie came in at three. The time she had originally planned to be there. Still, she was here and Mel was relieved to see her.

"Why don't you go upstairs for a bit? I can call you if we get busy. You look like shit."

"Well, thanks, Ell."

Ellie looked surprisingly fresh and breezy. Mel was about to head upstairs when Skiddy came in, shuffling his feet a bit and looking sheepish. He blushed deep red when he saw Ellie, even though he must have seen her arriving.

"Hi, Ellie. Hi, Mel."

"Hello again, Skiddy." Mel hid a grin.

"Thought I'd get the boss a coffee. He's been in a foul

mood today. Can I grab a flat white and a hot chocolate?"

"Sure." Ellie moved behind the counter to the coffee machine and Mel headed towards the stairs.

"You look nice today. That colour looks really good on you—" she heard Skiddy saying as she started up the stairs to the flat.

~

The next morning Mel found Jesse's socks, abandoned under her bed. They were black with pink polka dots. She picked them up gingerly from the floor and threw them into the washing machine with the tea towels and then later gave them to Kevin, along with the orange bedspread her mother had wrapped the sculpture in. She hadn't seen him for a few days and he told her he'd been hanging out down on the waterfront. He used to go out on a dinghy with his granddad when he was a kid and liked the smell of the salt air, but it was too cold down there in winter.

Ellie arrived in the afternoon with a pile of bags which she dumped on the floor by the counter.

"Christmas decorations," she explained, pulling tartan bows from one and a white dove from another. "What do you think?"

"Lovely."

The door jangled and they looked up to see Skiddy. As he seemed to every time he saw Ellie, he blushed.

"Knocked off early," he mumbled. "Thought I might get a

book for my mum for Christmas."

"Good, you can help me with the tree," Ellie told him. "Follow me."

Without waiting for a reply she led the way out to her car, Skiddy scuttling along behind her. They returned and he was lugging a large oblong box.

"Do you want help putting it up?" he asked hopefully.

"Well, sure, if you can spare the time. That would be great."

Skiddy proved to be pretty handy and the tree was up in no time. He even stayed to help decorate but could barely keep his eyes off Ellie, and Mel had to redo some of the positioning of his bows after he'd left. They'd had to practically push him out of the shop.

"That looks nice," Ellie said, observing their handiwork. "I'll wrap up some empty boxes with brown paper tomorrow and put them under it."

"And maybe a little present for your boyfriend," Mel teased. "There are some good young adult books that arrived today."

"Oh hush." Ellie threw an empty shopping bag at her.

"I slept with Jesse," Mel blurted. Ellie put down the wreath she was unwrapping and stared at her.

"You're kidding," she said in astonishment. "I thought you hated each other."

"We do, I mean, not hate, that's a very strong word. It's — we're always arguing, that's all. But then we made a truce. And had sex. And now we're back to arguing again ..." Mel trailed off with a sigh.

"Bloody hell, I mean, he is hot as hell though. All buff and grumpy." She stared at Mel. "Well?" she demanded.

"Well what?"

"What was he like? How hung is he? Give me all the dirt, bitch."

Mel laughed and pulled a face.

"Sadly, it was probably the best sex of my life. Like, really, really good. Doubly good — if you know what I mean."

"Damn," Ellie said. "Then I guess you need to make up. I hope you were safe?"

Mel sighed. "Yes, of course. But I don't think he actually likes me very much. He could barely look at me the next morning."

"Aww, babe, surely not. What's not to love about you? You're gorgeous, you have legs for ever and beautiful eyes. You're kind, good with kids and you can quote *Pride and Prejudice* like a pro."

"Thanks, El. I love you too."

"I know you do."

~

After Ellie left, Mel surveyed the bookstore. It looked like something from an old movie, she thought. All wood and books, softly lit up by the glowing fairy lights on the tree. Maybe she would get some glass jars and fill them with striped candy and jellybeans. She could put them up on the shelf behind the counter.

She looked at said shelf. Her mother's sculpture sat in glaring contrast to the rest of the shop. It stuck out like a very rude sore thumb. Or other unmentionable sticking-out things.

Mel decided to skip dinner and eat a Trumpet in bed. Maybe she'd reread *Pride and Prejudice*.

Chapter fourteen

*"How unfortunate, considering I have decided
to loathe him for eternity."*
Pride and Prejudice, Jane Austen

Friday and Saturday were the busiest they'd ever been. During the day they were flat out with Christmas shoppers. They offered free present wrapping and Ellie spent a lot of the day putting ribbons on book purchases. The evenings were also full, with lots of people coming in for pre-Christmas drink catch-ups and even a work function for a trendy start-up business on the Friday night which had Ellie and Mel run off their feet. But their bank accounts were looking more cheerful.

Mel had seen a lot of Skiddy, but nothing of Jesse. It was probably for the best, she kept telling herself. But she couldn't seem to stop herself looking out the window for him.

~

A new order of books had arrived and Mel had created a little display table with present suggestions on it. One of the books was a gorgeous glossy cookbook of Indian cuisine. She and Ellie had oohed and ahhed over the photos and decided they would do an Indian dinner on Tuesday and try out a couple of the recipes.

She was writing a shopping list of ingredients on Saturday in the lull before the evening crowd arrived, when Ellie came back. They'd run out of sticky tape and she'd walked down to the corner store to grab a roll.

"Well, that was weird," she announced as she came in the front door.

"Hmmm, what? What was weird?" Mel asked. Should she make the paneer, or buy it? she wondered.

"I just passed Claire," Ellie told her. "Walking down the road, all dolled up, and guess who she was with?"

"Who?"

"Nate," Ellie said dramatically. "They were holding hands. And when I said hello, Nate pretended not to see me. What a git."

So they were dating then. Mel wondered how long that had been going on. "Do you think he was dating her when he asked me out?"

"Probably," Ellie said. "He seems like a cheater."

"Poor Claire."

"Nah, those two are perfect for each other. Ooh, are we making garlic naan?" she asked, peering over Mel's shoulder at the cookbook.

"By 'we', do you mean me?" Mel replied drily.

"Well, you know you're a much superior cook to me, but I'll go get all the stuff if you want?"

"Deal," Mel said. "Shall we do a jalfrezi or a rogan josh, do you think?"

~

Sunday was the kids' reading hour so Mel had made ginger-bread men as well as raspberry muffins. She was sticking on candy buttons when there was a knock at the front door. It was only nine, but she guessed it might be her mother with the boys who were coming to the reading session.

It was Jesse. She stood in the doorway, staring at him in surprise.

He stared back. Finally he lifted a tool box in his hand. "Thought I'd fix that railing," he told her in a tight voice.

Mel stepped back wordlessly and let him in. He strode past her, his posture tense.

"It shouldn't take long, I'll be out of here before you open hopefully," he said without turning round.

"Umm, okay. Thank you so much," Mel finally said. "That's really nice of you."

"Yeah, well, it's dangerous," he said gruffly, "especially if you have kids around."

Mel tried not to take that as a rebuke on her babysitting skills.

"Can I get you a coffee?"

Jesse looked up at her. Shit. He'd shaved off his moustache. Mel couldn't stop staring at his face. He was really beautiful, she noted. Her girly bits did a little back-flip.

"—if that's okay," Jesse was saying.

"What? Oh, yes, sure," Mel blustered. She felt like she was bright red. She ran her hand through her hair. Did she have any makeup on? She wished she had put on a nicer top.

Going into the kitchen, she stared at the coffee machine blankly.

"Sorry," she headed back down the hall, "what did you want again?"

Jesse gave her a funny look. The corners of his mouth twitched like he was trying not to laugh.

"A black coffee, thanks."

She made them both a drink and took his back to him, along with a muffin. He was crouched down and his thighs strained in his board shorts. His T-shirt had ridden up and there was a thin strip of his back showing.

Why was that so hot? Mel thought, standing there like an idiot, looking at him.

She quickly set down the cup and plate and scuttled back down the hall as her mother came in with her nephews.

"Morning, Melly love." Marion ushered in the boys who ran up to hug Mel.

"Hi, guys." She bent down and squeezed them each in turn. "I've missed you."

"We went to the park," Flint told her. "There was a big poo on the slide."

"It was mud," Blade said dismissively.

"But it looked like poo," Flint insisted indignantly.

"It did," Marion agreed. "I had to sniff it first before I wiped it off."

"And we're going to help with the chickens later," Blade told her proudly.

"Geoff's building a bigger hutch," Marion explained.

"I get to pick up the first egg." Flint looked at Blade as he spoke. Blade rolled his eyes and Mel laughed.

"Do you want a gingerbread man?" she asked them.

"Person," her mother said.

Mel looked at her blankly. "What?"

"Person, darling. Gingerbread person. It's important not to force gender stereotypes on people, you know."

Mel laughed. "Good point," she agreed. "Maybe you could write 'Gingerbread person' on the blackboard menu for me?"

Jesse came back through as she was handing the biscuits to the boys. "Oh, hello, Jesse." Her mother fished out the chalk, giving him a smile. "Darling, you've got the tush round the wrong way," she announced as she spotted her sculpture. She turned the monstrosity round till the purple penis was more visible. Mel cringed.

"It's just a bit ... in your face ... like that," she told Marion.

"A bit prominent."

Marion laughed. "Oh, your father will love it when I tell him that."

Mel snorted her sip of coffee up her nose and stared at her mother in horror. "You mean — that's Dad?" she squeaked.

"Well, of course it is," Marion said calmly. "Who else did you imagine I got to model for me?" She looked over at Jesse as she spoke. "I don't suppose ..."

Jesse's eyes widened, and he blurted out, "Sorry, Mel, I need to pop out to my truck and grab a level." He placed the cup and plate on the bench and then when he caught Mel's eye, did a little laugh that he turned into a cough.

"Hello," said Flint in a little voice beside Jesse. He tugged on his shorts. "I want to pat the dog again."

Jesse looked down, then crouched down to Flint's level. "Hey, buddy," he said softly. "You can pat her, if it's okay with Aunty Mel and Nana."

"Marion," Mel's mother put in quickly. "Geoff and I don't believe in the use of society-created labels."

"Can I pat the dog too?" Blade asked Mel.

"Sure, buddy," she told him.

"Can you come?" he asked her, holding her hand.

"Okay. Come on, Flint, but be good and no running off." She stretched out her hand to him.

Flint took Jesse's hand instead and tugged him out the door.

"What's her name?" he asked when they got to the truck,

and Jesse lifted the dog down, holding her collar and telling her to 'Stay'.

"Scrubber," Jesse told him.

Mel's head spun round to stare at Jesse. "The dog's name is Scrubber?" she said, a little too loudly. My God, she was an idiot. She'd thought he'd been calling her a scrubber the first morning she'd met him, but it was the dog he'd called out to.

Jesse gave her a funny look and laughed. "Yeah, my kuia named her," he said, "' cause she was really naughty as a puppy."

"What's a kulia?" Flint asked as he hugged Scrubber round the neck. She was lapping up the attention, Mel noted, true to her name.

"Kuia is a Māori word," Jesse told him. "It means grandmother."

"Blade is Māori," Flint told him. "I'm not, 'cause my dad is a different one to his."

"Half Māori," Blade said, giving Scrubber's ear a scratch and laughing when she licked him back.

"Me too," Jesse told him. Blade smiled shyly at him.

"My teacher asked me if I want to join the kapa haka," he told Jesse.

"That's cool," Jesse replied. "That was my favourite part of school. Especially doing the haka."

"I want to join the kapa kapa too," Flint declared. Blade and Jesse laughed and Mel watched them both, with a weird fluttering in her stomach.

"I might need some help to fix the railing," Jesse told both boys. "Know anyone who could be my assistant?"

"ME, ME," they both shouted.

"Come on then." He handed Blade a level and gave Flint a tape measure from the cab. "We'd better get to work."

Both boys took off back to the shop with Jesse, talking over the top of each other, Flint doing a funny little skip. Mel watched them go, admiring Jesse's calves as he walked.

Bloody hell, get a grip, Melody Hawkins, she thought as she trailed behind them.

~

Eventually, Sophie arrived and Mel convinced the boys to reluctantly stop 'helping' Jesse and join the reading group. "Sorry," she mouthed as she dragged them away. Jesse gave her a wink and smiled. Damn he was cute without the moustache.

"I might pop out to the wholefoods store, if you don't mind?" Marion said. "I want to get some more wheatgerm and flaxseed, but I'll be back to get the boys before eleven," she promised.

"Bye, guys, I'll be back soon," she said to the boys.

"Bye, kuia," said Blade, and Flint, not to be outdone, blew her a kiss.

As soon as she left, Mel turned the sculpture back so the appendage was facing the wall. Behind her, Jesse did his booming laugh.

"Oh, shut up," Mel said, laughing herself. "I don't know how to get rid of the bloody thing. It's never going to sell."

"I'm almost done," he said. "I've glued the railing as well as using screws, so I'll tape everything up till it's dry. You can peel off the tape in the morning, okay?"

"Thanks so much," Mel said. "Really. I can't thank you enough, and coming on your day off too." Oh gawd, she thought, did that sound like she meant it to be sexual? She blushed. "Leave me the bill," she added quickly.

Jesse's smile faded. "Whatever." He stomped back to the stairs. What had she done now? she wondered.

~

Sophie was great with the kids and had them spellbound with her story reading. Mel even found herself stopping to listen a couple of times despite having either heard or read the stories herself dozens of times over. She did a couple of songs too and even Flint, who would normally be rolling around on the floor after twenty minutes, was completely engaged. They had eight kids and their parents, which wasn't a bad start, and hopefully word of mouth would mean they'd have more each week.

~

The shop got busy but luckily Ellie arrived just before twelve. Mel hadn't noticed Jesse leave but she looked up from serving a customer and his ute was gone. There was no bill.

Chapter fifteen

"I could easily forgive his pride, if he had not mortified mine."

Pride and Prejudice, Jane Austen

The cupcakes sat on her bench. Mel eyed them warily. She'd made them that morning planning to drop them off before she went to her yoga class. She looked across the road at Jesse's ute and sighed. You're being ridiculous, she told herself.

It's not like she made them for him after all. They were for Skiddy's birthday.

"Harden up, Mel," she said to the empty shop.

Right. She took a deep breath, picked up the container and went out the door.

Next door the art gallery was looking amazing. The interior was taking shape and the walls were half finished being plastered. Jesse was standing talking to a guy in white overalls, gesturing at the ceiling. He stopped mid-sentence when he saw her hovering in the doorway, then said something else before he wandered over.

"Hey," Mel said nervously. "I didn't want to come in without a hard hat." She gave him a small smile. Jesse stared at her, his eyes flicking down, then up. She looked down self-consciously, making sure she didn't have flour on her sports top.

"What's up?" he finally asked.

"Oh, I'm, I made these," she said stupidly, pushing the container at Jesse. "They're for Skiddy. For his birthday," she added.

"Right," Jesse said quietly. "Well, he's gone to the hardware store, but I'll give them to him when he gets back."

"Sure, sure, yeah, great. Well, I'd better get going, I have a class," she told him, waving her arm out towards the street like she was planning to do a downward dog position on the road or something.

God, he made her nervous. And horny. Must pick up some more batteries, she thought vaguely.

"Right, well, thanks," Jesse said.

Mel turned to leave. She must get her mind off this single track it was stuck on.

"Oh, and Mel?" he called after her.

She stopped and looked back at him, expectantly, a smile forming on her lips.

"Don't forget to take that tape off."

"Oh yeah, I, ah, yeah, I did," she replied. "See ya." She turned and walked down the street, feeling a bit pathetic.

~

She felt a lot better after yoga and a stroll through the cemetery by the gardens. Mel loved cemeteries and meandered through, sipping her juice and reading the headstones. The sun was out and it was a beautiful day. It really was true, she thought, you can't beat Wellington on a good day. She went down and ate a salad by the duck pond, watching them dip and dive, and enjoying sitting and doing nothing for a change. She headed home, thinking about a cold shower before she left for Fern's house to babysit.

It was about four and Skiddy was heading towards her with a box of beers in each hand.

"Happy birthday," she said when he got closer.

"Thanks, Mel," he smiled, "and thanks for the cupcakes. It's my shout today. Hey, do you want to come have a drink? And maybe Ellie too?" He lifted one of the boxes with a hopeful expression on his face. He was very cute.

"Thanks, but I'm off to my sister's shortly, and Ellie went to Martinborough yesterday for the night."

His face fell. "No worries, maybe another time?" he said hopefully.

"Maybe. Oh, hey Skiddy, can you tell Jesse I can pay him cash if he wants, for the stairs? If he would rather."

"Sure, I'll let him know," Skiddy said. "See ya."

Ellie was probably back by now but no point encouraging him.

~

She got to Fern's about six only to find her sitting at the kitchen table in her trackies sobbing into a wad of toilet paper while Blade and Flint played with the hose out on the back lawn, wearing nothing but their undies and shrieking loudly. There was no sign of Chase.

"What's going on?" Mel asked cautiously. Fern was a drama queen and she could turn on the waterworks at will.

"It's … it's a *boy*," wailed Fern.

Oh for God's sake, thought Mel.

"I had the scan." Fern blew her nose loudly. "I was so sure it was a girl. I even painted the room pink." She started to cry again.

"Well, traditionally, pink was actually a boy's colour," Mel told her. "How does Chase feel? Where is he anyway?"

"He's gone to do a gig," Fern told her. Chase was trying to make it as a DJ. Mel had been to one of his gigs before. He was awful. "He's happy," Fern wailed, "'cause he said he always wanted a son."

Mel looked out at the boys who were now digging a mud hole in the lawn. That was a bit sad, she thought, that Chase obviously didn't see them as his in any way. "Well, the boys will be happy too." She rubbed her sister's back gently. "They didn't want a sister, and look what good mates they are.

They'll love having a brother."

Fern sniffed.

"Was everything else good," Mel asked, "in the scan?"

"Yeah, he's fine. Gonna be a big one, like Blade. He's due on Anzac Day." She looked at Mel, her face all blotchy and her nose red. "Sorry," she said, "I don't mean to sound so miserable, but I really had my heart set on a girl."

Mel refrained from saying 'Maybe next time'. Instead she said, "Shall I make you a cup of peppermint tea?"

"Yes, please," said Fern. "I'm not going out now, but do you want to stay and have pizza with me and the boys?"

"Love to," Mel told her with a smile.

"And could you still bath the boys and put them to bed for me?" Fern pleaded.

"Sure. What are sisters for?"

~

It was late when she got home and she noticed Nate's Audi parked across the street but the lights were off in Claire's apartment. Mel climbed the stairs, the railing firm under her hand and smiled to herself. She got into bed and managed to read a chapter of her book before she fell asleep.

She dreamt she was being chased by a giant baby in an elf costume and fell into a pothole full of butter chicken. Jesse stood at the top and said, 'None of this would have happened if you'd worn a hard hat.' She woke up feeling both irrationally pissed off at him and hungry.

She was still a little miffed when he walked in the door the next morning.

Skiddy was there, getting a coffee for smoko and lingering at the wrapping table, trying to talk to Ellie.

"I'm not giving you a bill," Jesse declared without preamble. "I don't need a cashie under the table either. I did it to help out, okay? I don't need your bloody money. It was a favour."

Mel stared at him, mouth open. She was glad there was only Olive and one other customer in the shop, Skiddy excluded.

"Okay," she said slowly. "I'm sorry, I didn't want to presume that you'd do it for free, I mean, I didn't want to take advantage after we ..." she trailed off. "Sorry," she muttered again. Jesse looked a little contrite.

"You're welcome," he said more calmly. "Sorry for yelling."

Ellie glanced over as she farewelled the customer, looking intrigued.

"We're doing Indian tonight," she told Jesse. "Mel is a great cook. Why don't you join us? To say thank you," she added when Jesse looked like he was going to argue. He looked over at Mel.

"That would be good," she said softly. "You should come." He looked at her face for a bit, as if searching for something in her eyes.

"Okay, thanks."

They both smiled carefully.

"I love Indian," Skiddy announced behind them.

Jesse looked at him and raised one eyebrow dubiously. "You hate spicy food," he said. "You reckon the spicy KFC is too hot."

"Not Indian though," Skiddy insisted, blushing. "That's different."

There was an awkward pause. The only sound was Olive setting down her cup, and the rustle of a page being turned.

"Would you like to come too?" Mel said eventually. She tried to sound enthusiastic, and purposely didn't look Ellie's way. Skiddy looked thrilled.

Jesse grinned. "What time?" he asked.

"Any time after five is good," Mel told him. "I'm going to start cooking after lunch since Ellie's here. Come straight over when you knock off if you want, it won't be fancy."

The doorbell jangled and Colin came in, smiling at Mel and looking disdainfully at Jesse and Skiddy's work boots. Mel did a quick wave and shot out the back, leaving a disgruntled Ellie to deal with the lot.

Chapter sixteen

"This is an evening of wonders indeed."

Pride and Prejudice, Jane Austen

By the time Ellie put the closed sign up, Mel had cooked a chicken jalfrezi and a vegetable curry, made pickles and had a stack of garlic naan, ready to be reheated in the oven.

Ellie opened the bottle of wine she'd brought up from the shop and poured them each a glass. "The cooking smells have been wafting downstairs all afternoon." She went over to the stove and lifted a lid. "I'm starving."

Mel swatted her away and switched on the rice cooker.

"I hope there's enough for two guys. Do you think we should do some cheese as well?"

"Probably a good idea. I'll go and grab something from downstairs. I think there's an open jar of pickles as well. So anyway, about Jesse ..."

"What about Jesse?"

"Is he going to stay over tonight?" Ellie asked, with a smirk.

"I don't know, I mean we've only just got back to our truce. I kind of want to see how things go, I guess."

"You're thinking too much with your head as usual."

"Oh shut up. Go and get the cheese."

As Ellie went downstairs there was a knock on the door. She came back up followed by Jesse and Skiddy. Jesse handed her a bottle of wine — it was a nice one too — and Skiddy had brought a couple of craft beers and a packet of chips.

"I know they're not Indian," he mumbled.

"Neither is this," Ellie grinned, holding up the cheese. She emptied the chips into a bowl and quickly arranged cheese, pickles and crackers on a plate.

There was a bit of awkwardness as everyone decided where they were sitting; Skiddy and Mel on dining room chairs and Jesse and Ellie on the sofa.

"Smells good." Jesse stretched his long legs out in front of him. He was wearing a clean T-shirt — perhaps he kept one in the truck, Mel pondered — and it fitted nicely around his pecs.

"Have you guys ever been to India?" he asked.

"Not me," Ellie replied. "I love Indian food but my idea of a holiday is sitting in a bikini beside a pool, sipping a cocktail. Mel's the more adventurous one."

Skiddy had a slightly glazed look about him, as though he

were visualising Ellie in a bikini. He squirmed slightly.

"I've never been, unless you count pre-birth. Marion and Geoff went when she was pregnant with me," Mel told them. "Fern and I went to Peru with our parents when I was about four, and we lived in Rarotonga for a bit, but it's definitely on the bucket list. How about you?"

"No, not India, but my plan is to take time off next year and travel around South-East Asia." Jesse cut a piece of cheese and put it onto a cracker. "Probably around March or April, I reckon. I've always wanted to do it, so I figure why not bite the bullet and go?"

"I went to Brisbane with my mum when I was twelve," Skiddy chimed in.

"Well, that's more than I've done yet, mate," Jesse laughed.

Ellie told them about a trip she'd taken to Europe a few years ago and how she'd accidentally set off an alarm in a Parisian art gallery and almost been arrested. There had been a language barrier, so she'd decided next time she went away somewhere, she'd learn a few useful phrases.

"Good tip." Jesse raised his wine glass to her, "I should at least learn how to order a beer."

"And find a loo," Ellie added. "That's always handy."

Mel's little Formica table only seated two so she put all the food onto the coffee table and they loaded their plates.

"This is bloody delicious." Jesse tucked in enthusiastically.

"Really *hot*," Skiddy said, but he was looking at Ellie, and Mel wasn't sure whether he meant the food or not. His face had gone very red though.

"I'll get you a glass of milk if you like," she told him. "Apparently it helps."

"No, I'll be fine." He took a gulp of water. "Actually, maybe."

Jesse laughed and Skiddy went even redder, if that was possible.

Mel got the milk and Jesse asked if he needed a straw with it, which made Mel laugh.

"Oh, don't be mean," Ellie said gently. "Plenty of people can't eat spicy food, Aaron. My dad is actually allergic to chillies."

Skiddy shot her a grateful look.

"So, Mel, do you need to do some Christmas shopping? I could come in on Thursday morning if you like. I've only got Dad left to buy for so I'm pretty much done."

"Would you? That would be a lifesaver. I've barely started with the boys' presents. I'm a bit slack with the whole Christmas gift thing. We never really did Christmas as kids." She broke off some more naan. "Marion and Geoff didn't believe in spinning the whole Santa story to us, but since Blade and Flint have come along, they've completely changed their tune. I kind of feel envious of them; I always wanted a visit from Santa."

"Poor Mel," Ellie said. "I loved getting a stocking."

"It's only me and my mum," Skiddy told them. "My dad

lives in Australia. But my mum still gives me a Santa sack." He blushed again, and looked like he wished he hadn't said that.

"My mum does too," Jesse admitted, giving him a grin. "I have three sisters and it's bloody chaos at ours at Christmas. My youngest sister still tries to wake us up early to open the stockings, 'cause mum won't let us do them till we're all awake."

He told them how he lived with his oldest sister and the youngest was the only one still at home. They'd all be going back to Hawke's Bay a couple of days before Christmas, and his mum and aunties would cook a huge meal for the extended family.

"We'll be eating for days. I'll probably have to take up jogging when I get back to get rid of the extra beef."

Mel had a vision of Jesse in a small pair of jogging shorts.

"I'll go for a run with you if you like. You'll have to keep up though," she teased.

"I've seen you jogging past in the mornings sometimes," Jesse replied. "It wouldn't bother me if I had to be behind you, to be honest."

Ellie coughed awkwardly. "So, does anyone want another glass of wine?"

Jesse and Mel were still looking at each other and he seemed reluctant to tear his gaze away. "Not for me, thanks," he said, "I'm driving."

Mel wondered whether he was hinting about staying the

night. Or maybe that was wishful thinking on her part.

"Well, I'm going to leave my car here and Uber," Ellie announced.

"I'll open another bottle," Mel said, while Jesse said, "I've gotta take a leak."

They stood up at the same time and almost collided. Jesse reached out to steady Mel and she felt his hand on her bare skin, like a jolt of electricity shooting down her arm. Their eyes met again and he gave her a look which made her think he'd felt it too. He winked and his mouth twitched up, and she thought again how handsome he looked, clean-shaven.

There were leftover brownies from the shop for dessert and Ellie went downstairs and made coffees for everyone.

"Jesse, you live out near Wilton, eh?" Skiddy asked.

"Yep, why's that?"

"Could you give me a ride home? I'm on your way."

"Ahh, sure — you've only had one beer though, haven't you?"

Skiddy looked down at his feet. "It's after ten," he said.

Jesse raised his eyebrows in a question.

"I'm still on my restricted."

Jesse and Mel burst out laughing. Ellie kindly managed to contain herself.

"Sure, mate," Jesse told him. "I can give you a lift home too, Ellie, if you like. Save you the Uber."

Jesse and Skiddy insisted on doing the dishes and they all left soon after, thanking Mel for the amazing food. Jesse leant over to give her a kiss on the cheek, which missed. She'd moved her head and he got the corner of her mouth.

She watched reluctantly as he went downstairs behind Ellie and Skiddy.

Chapter seventeen

"... there seemed a gulf impassable between them."

Pride and Prejudice, Jane Austen

The 'Open' sign had barely been turned over the next morning when Claire arrived in a swish of skirts and expensive perfume. She was, as usual, perfectly coordinated with shoes and lipstick in the same shade. Mel was setting out the ginger slice and didn't like the look on her neighbour's face.

"Morning, Claire," she said as cheerfully as she could muster.

She'd been awake far too long last night, tossing and turning and thinking about Jesse. She'd had a weird dream where she was flying across an arid desert on huge bat-like wings, but they were only attached to her with duct tape.

Why did she have to start developing feelings for bloody Jesse? She was such a sap. One shag and now she was infatuated. How many times had Marion told her she didn't need a man to be happy? She was a failure as a feminist, she decided.

"Once again," Claire intoned, "I find myself arising to vehicles blocking my customers' access to my boutique."

Who said 'arising' anyway? Apart from maybe Colin, Mel mused. And what was with the French emphasis on 'boutique'? Mel considered herself a nice person, but something about Claire really irked the hell out of her. Her superior attitude? Or her always perfectly put together face? Mel had never seen her without makeup, even first thing in the morning, putting out the rubbish, or getting the mail. Maybe she slept in it. Either that or she never slept. Like a vampire.

"Hello?" Claire snapped.

Shit, she needed to stop with the paranormal books, Mel decided. And go to bed earlier.

"Sorry, Claire." Why was she always apologising? "But I don't even own a car. One is Ellie's. The other belongs to Ski—, to Aaron, a builder next door. You'll have to take it up with them."

Ellie chose that moment to swing in the door, a box full of lemons and a bag of wrapping paper in one hand. "I got a ride in with the boys," she announced, "and I swear Aaron was about to cum in his pants when I had to ..." She trailed off when she realised Mel wasn't alone.

"Hi, Claire, you look very glamorous and put together this morning."

Mel had always thought the expression 'looked down their nose' was weird and impossible, but Claire managed it. She looked over at Ellie and pursed her lips — like a cat's bum, Mel thought uncharitably.

"Please remove your car from my frontage," Claire requested.

Ellie was unfazed. "Well, I'll be gone in a half hour or so, Claire, in my car. But as I've mentioned before, it's public parking."

There was an icy silence.

Mel felt like things were escalating and she really didn't want to feature on an episode of *Neighbours at War* any time soon.

"Can I offer either of you a hot drink? I'm making a coffee for myself." She looked imploringly at Ellie, trying to telepathically request she be nice.

"Ooh, I'd love a chai," Ellie requested. "How about you, Claire, have you got time for a cuppa?"

Claire looked a little taken aback by the change in attitude. She put her hand up to her mouth, like she was shocked.

"Is that an engagement ring?" Ellie took hold of Claire's hand and examined it. Claire was wearing a large, princess cut diamond on a platinum band. She smiled. It was odd seeing her smile, Mel thought. It didn't really suit her, looking out of place on her normally expressionless face.

"Yes, my boyfriend — well, I suppose he's my fiancé now — proposed on Saturday," she told them smugly.

"Nate Carmichael?" Mel asked.

"Yes." Claire smiled again. "I suppose you've heard the name? The family *are* very well established. His parents and mine have been firm friends for many years. They are, of course, thrilled." She admired her ring. "It will be quite the society wedding," she added with puffed up satisfaction.

"Lovely," Mel murmured. Should she say anything about Nate and her? she wondered. Talk about awkward. But it was really only one date. And the flirting was definitely one-sided and something she'd never encouraged. Not even a little bit. Still, she had a funny feeling Claire wouldn't see it like that.

"How long have you dated for?" Ellie asked.

"Almost two years, so a perfectly timed engagement. I imagine we'll get married next summer."

Mel and Ellie both smiled fakely.

"Lovely," Mel repeated.

"Well." Claire seemed oddly embarrassed to have let go of her bitchy attitude, even for a moment. "Please do remove the cars. My clientele need to be able to park as close as possible to the boutique," she said as she left.

Ellie and Mel looked at each other. "*Two* years," Mel said.

Ellie started unloading the wrapping paper. "Should we say something? It sort of feels like we should, but she's such a bitch."

"I dunno. What is there to say? 'Hey, Claire, your fiancé and I had dinner, and he seems a bit sleazy.'"

"True." They sipped their drinks.

Ellie grinned. "So, are we going to talk about the heat in the kitchen last night?"

Mel laughed. "What with you and your toy boy?"

"Oh, shut up." Ellie threw a lemon at her, which Mel miraculously caught.

"Aaron is a sweetie though. I feel bad. It's awful having an unrequited crush."

"Yes, schoolboy crushes suck."

Ellie gave her the finger. "Anyway, I was talking about you and Jesse and you know it. Why don't you just shag him again?"

Mel sighed. "Why did he have to shave off his moustache? He's so much hotter now."

Ellie laughed. "Plus he's hung like a donkey, right?" she said, fishing for gossip.

Mel did the finger back. "You know size doesn't matter — it's all to do with technique." She got up and took their empty cups to the sink. "I was thinking we should have a little Christmas party?" she said over her shoulder. "Invite some locals, some regular customers, you know, to say thanks for supporting us."

"Subject change noted, but yeah, that sounds good. Maybe invite some of the wine reps I use too. Mum and Dad will come, and Marion and Geoff, I'm guessing? Can we do it on Christmas Eve, do you think? Then I could go back with them to the winery."

Mel thought for a bit. "I guess so, we're open right up till then anyway."

"Let's write some lists before we get busy. Make a budget." Ellie got up to find a notebook. "And I'm in no rush to leave," she said with a look over at Claire's and an evil little grin.

~

After lunch, Jesse arrived, carrying Mel's cupcake container.

"Sorry, keep forgetting to give this back."

"Thanks."

"Thanks again for dinner. It was great."

"My pleasure. It was fun."

Mel cleared a table and took the cups to the kitchen.

"Actually." Jesse followed her through. "I was hoping you could help me pick out a book?"

"Oh, of course. Sure." Mel wiped her hands and gestured back at the shelves.

"Who's it for? You? Or a gift?"

"A gift. For my ... boy. He's nearly four."

Mel felt like a cartoon coyote who'd been hit with an anvil. He had a kid? Not that that was a big deal, she told herself. She was just surprised. He hadn't mentioned having a kid. Where was the mum? Christ, she hoped they weren't still together, although that was mean. The poor kid probably would prefer that. Oh shit, what if he was married?

"Umm, okay," she managed, her voice sounding all weird and breathy. Get it together, she told herself. You had sex once. Drunk sex. Big deal. Be a professional.

"So, all our kids' books are over here," she said, sounding a bit prim, leading him to a small section of the store that they used as a children's area. "If he's close to four, he's probably going to want either a basic picture book or a story you or his, umm, mum, can read to him." She pulled down several books, including *The Very Hungry Caterpillar*, *The Gruffalo* and *The Little Yellow Digger*. God, her hand was shaking.

"Mel," Jesse said, but the bell rang with a customer and Mel shoved the pile of books at him.

"Have a look and see if any of these would suit." She didn't look at his face as she moved away, thankful for the reprieve.

Ellie was there, so when Jesse came up to the counter, Mel took some extra napkins to another customer so she could avoid having to serve him. She had a toilet break while Ellie wrapped the book for him, sitting on the lid of the loo, head in her hands while she tried to pull herself together. She was being a drama queen, she told herself.

He was gone when she came back out.

"Wow," Ellie said, her voice a little sharp.

"What?"

"I hate to say it, Mel, but you seemed a little judgmental."

"What? No, I was surprised, that's all."

"Okay, if you say so. You do realise that plenty of people have kids?"

Was she being judgmental? Mel thought. What was it about Jesse that made her act so awful? So superior. It really wasn't like her. She felt terrible. She should think of a way to apologise, again, but she wasn't sure how.

Chapter eighteen

"Whatever bears affinity to cunning is despicable."

Pride and Prejudice, Jane Austen

Mel sat wrapping some more empty boxes to put under the tree while Ellie put away the clean coffee cups. It was just after five, but still a beautiful sunny day with no wind at all. The fan whirred overhead and she sang along to the Christmas mix they had playing in the background. She was contemplating going to the beach to swim on her day off when she realised someone was there. Jesse leant in the doorway watching her. He was grinning.

"I see why your mother called you Melody," he said. He was definitely being smart. Mel could not sing to save herself, much to her disgust. She poked out her tongue.

"We can't all be crooners."

He grinned. "I came over 'cause I wanted to explain about

the kid."

"Oh, you don't owe me an explanation, it's your business." She could feel herself blushing.

"I know, but I wanted to. I'm not married, if that's what you were thinking. I swear, I'm single. It's just ... it's a bit of a long story." He fiddled with the bell above his head. Her eyes went to his stomach where his T-shirt had slid up. Her cheeks felt like they were glowing.

"I thought maybe we could have dinner? I know you work most nights, but maybe Sunday? If you're free?"

"Umm, yeah, sure. That sounds good." She'd shredded the end of the string into a tassel, she realised.

"Okay, cool, ummm, I better go, Scrubber's getting hot." He gestured towards his truck, where the dog was sitting panting on the flat-bed. "I'll see ya."

The bell clanged again as he left, and Mel realised she was grinning like a loon.

Ellie laughed, and she jumped. She'd forgotten she was even there.

"You two are so cute."

~

Thursday and Friday were crazy busy. She and Ellie got into a good rhythm with swapping from coffee making, serving at the book counter and taking breaks. The weather was amazing and the outdoor table was constantly occupied.

Her mother came in on Saturday and helped them out,

clearing tables and wrapping books. She turned out to be a great saleswoman too, convincing people to buy books on all sorts of topics as gifts. It helped that she was a bit of a Jill-of-all-trades, so she knew a little bit about most things. She sold books on beekeeping, preserves, hiking, and horticulture. Sales were up and life was pretty good.

~

Sunday morning Ellie was on, so Mel walked to Zealandia and wandered around under the cool canopy of trees, bird watching.

She finished off the last of her Christmas shopping. Everyone was getting a book, obviously. And she had made her parents some beeswax wraps and some marinades. They preferred a home-made gift and were the least materialistic people Mel knew. She picked up a body balm for Fern that was supposed to be good for stretch marks and a pair of funky earrings for Ellie. She got the boys some walkie-talkies.

Walking down to the waterfront later she sat and sipped an iced coffee and watched people jumping off the pier. She'd never done it herself, but it looked fun and it was definitely hot enough.

Her phone dinged with a text. It was Nate.

Hey sexy, how's it?

She didn't reply.

While she walked home, she thought about Jesse. He came across as a nice guy, she thought, and she wondered why she'd been so quick to judge him. It wasn't like her parents had raised her to think she was better than anyone else. Geoff had drilled into the girls to be respectful of everyone, be it the President or a janitor.

He'd come into the shop late Friday afternoon to ask if she liked Thai, and said he'd pick her up at six on Sunday if that was okay. Skiddy had been behind him, peering into the front window as he went past, hoping to see Ellie, and Jesse had said, "And no, Skiddy, you're not coming with us," before winking at her, leaving her laughing as he drove off with a wave.

Skiddy had been in both days, apparently to buy books for Christmas gifts, but leaving without anything when Ellie had been too busy to serve him.

"That little cutie pie is smitten," Marion had said, making Ellie cringe. "Nothing wrong with a younger man," she added. "Think of all the things you could teach him, before he learns it all wrong."

"Not going to happen," Ellie said firmly.

Mel showered and changed into a short pantsuit and some dressy sandals.

She poured herself a glass of pink gin and soda and add-ed some ice cubes and raspberries and sat outside at the wrought iron table to drink it. It was lovely — cool and refreshing.

She hadn't seen Kevin for a while, she realised, looking across at his favoured doorway. She hoped he was okay.

Jesse pulled up in a red Mazda and got out to greet her.

"Where's the ute?"

"It's a bit grubby for a date. I did a swap with my sister. You look nice."

"Thanks, so do you." He was wearing khaki dress shorts and a shirt with pineapples on it.

"Do you want to get going now? Or can I make you one of these." Mel waved her glass at him.

"I'm good, thanks, but no rush to finish it." He dropped down onto the other seat and they sat in the evening sun, while Mel sipped.

"How much longer will you be working on the gallery?"

"We're almost done. It's the usual story though. Held up by the painters, who've been held up by the electrician, who's closing down next week for the holidays. It's the same every year. All the suppliers close and we're left sitting round with our fingers up our bums." He drummed his fingers on the table. "What about you? Are you closing over Christmas?"

"Working right up, then taking the stats. We're too new to shut for too long, and since I'll be here, I may as well stay open," Mel shrugged. "Ellie's going to go back and forth to

Martinborough a bit over the summer, to help her dad with wine tours. Her brother Brandon does a lot but it's a busy time for them."

Mel finished her drink and held up the empty glass. "I'll put this inside and be right out."

~

The restaurant was a popular one and busy, but Jesse had pre-booked and the waiter seated them straight away.

"I love Thai food." Mel scanned the menu. "Ohh duck, I can never go past duck."

"Me too. Shall we share some dishes?"

They spent a bit of time going over the options, and ordered.

"Look, Mel, I don't want to just jump into my sad and sordid past, but I really want to explain about Tama."

"Okay, but first, I want to apologise for my reaction when you told me. It was rude and I'm sorry if I came across as judgy."

"Okay, well, thanks."

"So Tama, that's his name?"

"Yeah. So, I met Reia when I was in my last year at school and we went out on and off for a year. When I left school and started my apprenticeship, we kind of dated again then we broke up, saw other people for a couple of years, but we got back together and she kinda moved in."

Jesse took a sip of his beer while the waiter put cutlery and plates down for them.

"She got pregnant when we were young. It wasn't planned. Tama was born in February and we were pretty happy."

Mel waited while he gathered his thoughts.

"When he was almost two, I cut my hand at work and I came home early. Found her and my best mate from school in bed." He looked at her and shrugged. "The old cliché."

Shit, Mel could see it was still a bit raw. She reached out and put her hand on top of his for a minute.

"That sucks. I'm so sorry."

"Oh, it gets worse," Jesse said with a dry laugh. He ordered Mel another drink as the waiter went by.

"Turns out, they'd been shagging since high school. It wasn't till my mum questioned it that I even thought about the fact that Tama might not be mine."

"Oh no." Mel felt herself welling up.

"I made her do a DNA test," he told her. "In a way, I wish I hadn't."

He looked so sad, and Mel had to sip her drink to get rid of the lump in her throat.

"Anyway, long story short, he wasn't mine, and now she and Ant are playing happy families back in Hawke's Bay."

"God, I'm so sorry," Mel said in a choked-up voice. Jesse looked at her and gave her a sad smile.

"Hey, it's okay, I'm okay."

The food arrived and they spent a few minutes in silence as the plates were placed on the table.

"So, my mum was real upset and I couldn't handle living in the same town, so I got a job working for Pete, moved into my big sister's spare bedroom, and took Scrubber with me."

"Do you see Tama still?" Mel asked.

"Nah, that's the shit part. She won't let me. I don't have any legal rights, so ..." He trailed off. "It's just been hard to let it go, ya know? He still feels like my son."

Bloody hell, Mel was going to start sobbing soon. She sniffed and Jesse looked at her and gave a little laugh. Not his big booming one though, and she suddenly desperately wanted to hear that laugh.

"Aww, you big softy," he said gently. "Anyway, let's tuck in, the spring rolls look bloody good."

"Yeah, okay. But I think you're amazing. His biological dad or not."

"Thanks, Mel."

They loaded up their plates.

"Sorry to be such a downer," he told her. "I just — I wanted you to know that I wasn't some deadbeat dad or anything. I like you, Mel, and I felt like I should tell you."

Mel stopped with her fork halfway to her mouth.

"I like you too."

~

The conversation stayed lighter the rest of the meal.

They talked about Thailand and some of Jesse's tentative travel plans. He told her about his parents and his sisters.

The second youngest was at university in Palmerston North and the youngest still lived in Hawke's Bay. His mum was a caregiver and his dad worked on an oil rig, so he was away most of the year. Jesse was planning to go back and see them for Christmas. They lived quite rural and had a big section, and he would take Scrubber pig hunting while he was there, which she loved.

They talked a bit about the art gallery Jesse's crew were working on.

"I hope it does well," Mel said. "It'll be good for us to have it next door, I think. I'm going to stock some more art books and do a display when they open. Lure them in, hopefully."

"He's got some nice pieces, looking at his catalogue," Jesse said, then looked sheepish. "Not that I really know anything about art."

"I think we all like what we like with art though, don't we?" Mel said. "And my mother's work is *not* what I like." Jesse grinned.

"So you don't imagine it will sell?"

"No. It's just so awful, but I know she'll notice if I take it down. I already had to shell out fifty bucks for the painting." She gave him a quick rundown and explained about the subject matter and Jesse laughed loudly.

There it is, Mel thought with a smile.

They were too full for dessert. Jesse insisted on paying the whole bill, despite Mel offering to go halves. They got back in the car and he drove her home.

As they pulled up, they saw Colin, locking up his store. Mel gave him a wave as they drove past, pulling up to the bookshop and parking behind a sliver Audi.

"Ergh, Nate," she pulled a face. "He's such a slimeball."

Jesse scowled. "I hate that douche."

"It's Claire I feel sorry for," Mel told him. "They're engaged."

Jesse looked at her for a long moment. "I don't know if I should say anything," he said.

"What?"

"It's just — that guy is bad news. You don't want to get caught up with him."

"Well, he's my landlord, so I kind of am. Plus he's a wanker. He tried to get into my pants even though he and Claire have been together for ages."

Jesse's face looked murderous at the mention of her pants and Mel laughed a bit, feeling flattered.

"Calm down, I didn't even kiss him."

"Sorry, I guess I only like the idea of me getting into your pants."

Mel gave him a cheeky grin. "I doubt they'd fit you." Man, she loved his laugh.

"Seriously, though, he's not a good guy. He's a coke addict."

"Really? How do you know that?"

"Okay, look ... he dated my little sister, okay. Back in her first year of uni when she was at Vic, doing a law degree. She was totally in love with the prick." Jesse looked at her, then he sighed.

"She's real smart, but she was young. She thought he was handsome and he seemed really into her. She hadn't had a real boyfriend before, you know? She's ... naive. Innocent. She doesn't even drink."

Mel nodded.

"One night they got pulled up by the cops. Nia was driving Nate's car and she didn't stop fully at a stop sign. Anyway, Nate got a bit lippy with the cops, and they searched the car. They found a gram of coke in Nia's handbag."

"Fuck."

"Exactly. They took them both down to the station. Nate was resisting arrest and it was a bit of a shitstorm. She was interrogated and they did blood tests. Hers came out clean. And the coke wasn't hers."

"Of course not. So Nate put it in there?"

"Yeah. Turns out he had a bit of a rap sheet, been given a diversion before. Bit of drunk and disorderly, that sort of stuff. But he denied it was his. They let her off eventually, but the damage was done. Word spread she'd been done for coke and she ended up leaving uni. That's why she went to Palmy. She's doing a social work degree now."

"And what about Nate?"

"His dad's a pretty well connected guy and they've got money. He was never charged that I know of."

"Bloody hell."

"Just be really careful with him, okay?"

Chapter nineteen

"Have you any other objection than your
belief of my indifference?"

Pride and Prejudice, Jane Austen

"Well, I suppose I should let you go," Jesse said after a bit. They were still sitting in the Mazda, the windows fogging slightly.

"Right, okay." Mel reached for the door handle, then turned to look at him. He was staring at her legs. "Unless, I mean, we didn't get coffee at the restaurant?"

Jesse grinned. "Coffee would be good."

They got out of the car and she fumbled in her shoulder bag for the keys, then let them in the back door.

"I'll have to heat up the machine."

"Mel."

"Yes?"

"I don't really want a coffee."

And then he kissed her again.

After they broke apart, both heavy breathing a bit, Mel reached out and rubbed her finger along Jesse's top lip.

"Have I mentioned how much better this looks?"

"It was for Movember," he insisted. Mel laughed. She took his hand and pulled him up the stairs.

~

God, he was fantastic in bed, she thought later. They were both a little sweaty and the fan wasn't doing much to help. They lay on top of the covers, and she ran her hand down his chest, touching all the ridges and grooves of his muscles, feeling sticky and content.

"So, the truce is back on?"

Jesse laughed, his chest rumbling. He rolled over and bit her gently on the side of her neck, making her shiver.

"Definitely. In fact, I think I surrender."

Then he kissed her again.

~

Mel had the next day off and Jesse decided to take a day off with her, texting Pete to let him know. They talked about going to the beach perhaps or a hike. For once, Mel had a chance to sleep in. She didn't. She woke up at about six as usual, needing a pee, and when she got back, Jesse was awake, looking all tousled and rumpled and watching her pad across the floorboards in the nude.

"Dammit, woman," he said with an appreciative groan. "Get over here."

~

Morning sex was the best, she thought, as she dozed back off later, admiring the contrast of their skin tones as they spooned, his arm slung across her, and his firm body pressed into her back.

~

They spent the day in bed. The only time they got dressed was when the Uber Eats driver arrived with their food. As they sat on the bed eating, Jesse leant over and kissed her again.

"Why a bookstore?" he asked.

"I've always loved books. I think because we never settled anywhere for long, I found it hard to keep up friendships as a kid. Books were my friends and every new school I went to, I'd live in the library for the first week till I got my bearings a bit. I always thought I'd become a librarian," she told him with a grin.

"Ohh, I bet you'd have been hot," Jesse laughed. "So, what's your favourite book? Or author?"

"*Pride and Prejudice*. Jane Austen. Why, what's yours?"

"Probably Stephen King. But I loved *Pinot and Pūhā*," he

told her.

Mel was surprised to find he'd read it, although it did have hunting in it.

"When did you read that? In school?"

Jesse looked a bit sheepish. "Nah, I read it in July," he said. "After you put up the sign."

"That's very adorable," she told him, kissing him again. "Did you know I worked for George Henry? That's why we have this place really. He was a grumpy old prick, but he was an amazing writer and I loved him. When he died, he left me some money. I have his first ever published book under the glass counter downstairs. That's my pride and joy, that book."

"Sounds like he was an important man to you."

"Yeah, he was. He'd have liked you."

They ate for a bit, grinning at each other and nudging feet.

"So, are we dating then?" he asked her quietly. She thought he sounded hopeful.

"Yeah. Yeah, I think we are," she replied, pinching one of his halloumi fries.

Chapter twenty

"My good opinion once lost, is lost forever."

Pride and Prejudice, Jane Austen

Mel was in the back storeroom the next day during a morning lull when she was startled by a movement in the doorway. It was Nate, leaning against the door frame observing her. Her good mood disappeared immediately, as she thought of what Jesse had told her about Nate and his sister.

"Nate. How can I help you?" she asked coldly.

"I'm here on business actually. I wanted to let you know I'm increasing the rent on the building, starting in the New Year, so don't go and spend all your Christmas profits at once now, will you?" He grinned, but Mel didn't return his smile. She stood from where she'd been crouching and turned to face him.

"Okay, well, for a start, I'm pretty sure you can't do that.

You're not allowed to increase the rent so soon into the tenancy and secondly, you really should be giving me notice if you need to pop in to see us, rather than turning up out of the blue like you've been doing."

His smile was replaced by an ugly scowl. Mel didn't know why she'd ever thought he was good looking.

"You're open now, aren't you?" he sneered.

"We are open but it doesn't seem like you've come in to buy anything."

"Yet this is the first time you've complained about it. You seemed pretty hot for me earlier, didn't you?"

"I'm sorry, but I don't think I ever gave you that impression. If I did, I certainly didn't mean to."

"Come on, don't give me that. Don't play dumb with me." He took a step towards her and Mel started to feel distinctly uncomfortable. She stepped back and almost tripped over the box she'd been unpacking.

"You know you want it. Put the closed sign up and we'll go upstairs."

"Ah, no. What do you think your fiancée would think about that?"

He paused for a second, looking annoyed. "Why would she have to know?"

He took another step forward and then as Mel started to panic, there was a loud jangle as the door opened. A voice called out, "Hello? Mel, Ellie?"

Nate looked around wildly, then turned and strode angrily

out of the shop. Mel followed, to find Olive standing at the counter. She'd never been so pleased to see her.

"Sorry, I hope you weren't busy."

Mel took a few seconds to calm herself, mustering up a smile.

"Not at all, Olive. You're in late today, I thought maybe you weren't coming."

"I've been doing a Christmas reading at the rest home where I work. Most of the residents slept through it, to be honest. Perhaps I should have gone with *Fifty Shades of Grey* instead of Dickens."

Mel laughed. Olive had quite a sense of humour when you got to know her. "Can I get you a pot of tea?"

Mel could still feel her heart thumping erratically in her chest after her encounter with Nate, but tried to compose herself.

Ellie arrived looking a bit flustered.

"Bloody hell, I just saw Nate tearing away like a maniac. His car almost collected me crossing the road. What did he want anyway — I saw him coming out of the shop — was he drunk or something?"

"Maybe the 'or something'— tell you about it later."

"Christ, I'm rattled. Do you think it's too early for a Christmas brandy?"

"A bit, yeah. I'll make you a coffee if you like and you can have a rum ball instead."

"I suppose that will have to do. Are you okay? You

look pale."

Mel glanced over to where Olive now had her nose buried in a book and gestured to Ellie to follow her into the back section of the shop. She told her about the visit with Nate, and about what Jesse had told her.

"Bloody hell, Mel, what a wanker. He sounds like he's a bit unhinged."

"When I mentioned Claire, he didn't seem at all bothered that he was trying to hit on me when I knew about her. He was really giving off creepy vibes."

"I almost feel sorry for her, the silly tart."

"I know. Do you reckon I should say something to her?"

Ellie tapped her hand on a table and looked thoughtful. "I don't know how we couldn't, in all good conscience. Especially with the drugs stuff."

"It doesn't really solve our problem of how we're going to deal with him though. Is there somewhere we can make a complaint?"

"Everything's been going so well that I hate to think of upsetting things but I think we'll have to."

"We might have to speak to a lawyer in the New Year. That's not going to be cheap though."

Ellie put a comforting hand on Mel's shoulder. "I'll make the coffee, shall I? Do those rum balls have actual rum in them?"

As they returned to the front of the shop, Mel noticed Colin striding purposefully past the window.

"Great, just what I need," she muttered to Ellie. "Why do all the nutcases seem to be drawn to me?" She ducked down out of sight behind the counter, suddenly noticing the Christmas wrapping paper needed reorganising.

"Apart from Jesse. He definitely seems like he's got it all going for him," Ellie chuckled. "Hello, Colin, how are you today?"

"Very well, very well, can't complain. Actually, maybe you could help me; I need to find a book for my aunt. She's a very cultivated woman of great intelligence, so I'd like to get her something that would challenge her mind."

"I see, of course." Ellie glanced down at Mel who mouthed something at her but stayed crouched where she was.

"Coward," Ellie whispered, and then to Colin, "Perhaps a classic?"

"Oh no, I imagine she's already read every classic that would be worthy. Maybe a revered modern novel, if there is anything that could come close to that."

Ellie didn't have the book knowledge that Mel had but she led Colin over to a selection of books. "How about *The Luminaries*?"

Olive looked up from where she sat nearby. "Sorry to interrupt, but I'd say if the gentleman's aunt is such an erudite woman, she may have already read that novel. Could I be so bold as to make a suggestion?"

"By all means, Olive, I'd be thrilled if you did. Colin, have you met Olive?"

"I don't believe I've had the pleasure."

Olive delicately shook his proffered hand and Ellie retreated gratefully, leaving them to discuss a suitable book for his aunt.

She sniggered on her way to the back office to do the accounts, as she saw Mel still cowering behind the counter, trying to duck waddle to the back room without being seen.

"Ah, Melody," Colin said as he spotted her. "Whatever are you doing? That doesn't look overly ladylike."

"Lost a contact," Mel told him with an impressively straight face.

Chapter twenty-one

*"Do not consider me now as an elegant female,
intending to play you, but as a rational creature,
speaking the truth from her heart."*

Pride and Prejudice, Jane Austen

Things got busy, and Ellie insisted she needed to go out and drop off Christmas gifts to the wine reps. Mel was feeling a little overwhelmed until Olive came up to the counter.

"Tell me if it's presumptuous," she said, "but I could help?"

"Olive, I could kiss you," Mel said.

They worked together in a nice easy harmony, Mel working the cash register and making the food while Olive assisted people with book selections, cleared tables and even ran some orders down to be posted. Mel was rather impressed at how quickly Olive got into the flow of things, and said so when things finally slowed down a little.

"My father had a restaurant," Olive told her. "I'm used to customer service."

"Does he still own it?"

"No, he was hopeless with the books," Olive said. "That's sort of why I got into accounting actually, but he'd gone into liquidation before I qualified. He died not long after and it was just Mum and me."

"Well, I can't thank you enough, and you must let me pay you," Mel said, but Olive shook her head. "At least take some books?" Mel offered. Olive thought about that for a bit and finally agreed to take two.

"Thank you, I was going to buy a few extra for the holidays. But I'm happy to help any time, really. I love coming here. It's my favourite place."

Ellie arrived back, carrying a box of wines and several boxes of fancy chocolates. Mel reached in and picked out a box.

"Take these too, Olive," she insisted. "I couldn't have managed without you."

It was a little bit of a dig at Ellie, but it seemed to sail over her head.

They closed at five and Ellie tidied the shop while Mel cleaned the coffee machine and made a batch of pastry for her Christmas mince tarts. Claire's shop was open until six and Mel waited until then before she went to see her.

Mel could see Claire through the glass door, steaming a

garment, and knocked to let her know she was there.

"Hello, I'm actually closed, you know," she said as she reluctantly unlocked the door.

"Claire, do you mind if I come in? There's something I really need to talk to you about."

Claire looked for a second as though she was going to decline but then silently stepped aside to let her enter. Mel glanced around the shop. It was minimalist but really rather lovely, with white painted floorboards, neat racks of expensive-looking clothing, gilded chairs upholstered in pale lilac chintz and a glass table with a large display of white lilies giving the shop a classy look. She was aware Claire was waiting for her to speak.

"It's about Nate," she said.

Claire screwed up her pert nose as though smelling something unpleasant.

"I'm not sure how to say this, but I'm just going to put it out there. Ever since we opened he's been trying to hit on me. We even went out for dinner one night but I was completely unaware he had a girlfriend. Well, fiancée, now."

"I doubt he meant it in a romantic way," Claire scoffed. "He's your landlord, isn't he?"

"It wasn't a business dinner, Claire, he wouldn't have invited me back to his house for coffee if it was, would he?"

"And did you go back to his house for coffee?"

"No, I didn't."

"It's quite possible you misunderstood. I'm sure he didn't

mean it how you thought he did. Nate's a very attractive man. Women are always throwing themselves at him. It's a bit tiresome for him, truthfully."

"There's more. I've heard he could have a bit of a drug problem."

Claire scoffed. "You *heard*? Heard this where? You really should be careful about spreading gossip, Melody. It's not a good look."

"I just ..."

"I don't know why you want to cause mischief. You and your friend have been nothing but trouble since you came here and opened your little ... shop." Claire strode to the door and opened it forcefully. "I'd like you to go now, please."

"Claire, please, let me ..."

"I'm not discussing this further. Either you're jealous of Nate and me or you're a troublemaker, but you need to leave. Goodbye."

"I'm sorry, I'm only trying to ..."

"Please leave now," Claire hissed through gritted teeth.

Well, she'd tried, Mel thought, as she locked her own shop door behind her and set the alarm. She wasn't sure what more she could say to Claire to convince her. Hopefully she'd find out what kind of person Nate was before she actually married him. Or Mel could try writing her a letter, which would probably end up tossed in the rubbish bin.

~

There was a text from Jesse asking how her day had been, even though he'd been over earlier for coffee and to check the railing was still holding out okay. They'd had a snog in the hallway but he'd had to leave as he'd promised a friend of his sister's he'd fix some rotten floorboards.

He'd also sent a photo of Scrubber, gazing mournfully into the camera lens.

Smiling, she texted him back:

Better now xx

Chapter twenty-two

"I must learn to be content with being happier than I deserve."

Pride and Prejudice, Jane Austen

On Wednesday while Mel did another online book order, she added a copy of Lonely Planet's South-East Asia travel guide to the cart to give Jesse for Christmas.

She got distracted buying a squeaky pig and a pair of reindeer ears for Scrubber. She forgot to cut up the ginger slice and hadn't turned on the coffee machine when the first customer arrived. After that, it felt like she was on the back foot all day.

It was stinking hot. She had her period and she was feeling a bit over it all. When her mother rang to see if she wanted any help that weekend, she felt oddly teary.

"What's the matter, honey?" Marion asked, ever perceptive. "You sound a bit off?"

"Nothing really," Mel said truthfully. "Just a bit off my stride today. I'll be fine."

"Why don't I come over tomorrow and give you a break?" Marion offered. "You could go for a run, or take a nap, or do some meditation. Perhaps your chakras are blocked? Have you been eating too much meat?"

For some reason that made Mel think of Jesse and she laughed.

"Thanks, Mum, but really, I'm fine. I'll have an early night and be back to normal tomorrow. Besides, aren't you guys flat out at the moment?"

"Well, we've been a bit under pressure to finish the latest build, but Geoff seems to think we'll be okay. He's been doing a lot of late nights and early mornings, but it's not stuff I'm much help with, I'm afraid."

"He should hire someone to help."

"Yes, probably, but you know Geoff. He doesn't suffer fools and he says he'd rather do it himself than work with anyone incompetent. We'll muddle along."

The bell on the door rang again.

"I'd better go, Ellie's getting swamped."

"All right, love, ring me if you need me, otherwise I'll see you Saturday."

~

When Jesse came over after work to say hi, she was flagging.

"You all right?" he asked her, his forehead creased

with worry.

"Yeah, I'm fine, just cramps."

"Ah, right. Hey, listen, want to go to the beach this week-end? I thought we could take Scrubber, and a picnic maybe?"

"I'd love to," Mel said wistfully, "but I'm working."

"I can cover for you Sunday," Ellie told her, shamelessly listening in.

"Really? I feel bad though, you did last Sunday."

"Yeah, but I'll be off heaps next month, so I owe you. Go, be all romantic and mushy."

Mel gave her a grateful smile and the finger.

"Sweet, but I better go," Jesse said. "I left Skiddy sanding the floor. He says hi, by the way." He gave Ellie a wink and Mel a quick kiss and left.

When he popped back at four-thirty, he was carrying a shopping bag and he handed it over, kissed her again and left, off to pick up some fittings before the supplier closed for the day.

He'd been to the supermarket and the chemist. There were painkillers, a wheat bag, a big bar of chocolate and some peanut m&m's, plus three different types of tampons.

Ellie peered over Mel's shoulder at her stash.

"Now that man is a keeper. How many guys do that?"

Mel laughed. "Three sisters, remember?"

~

As with any new relationship, Mel found herself thinking

constantly about Jesse and they spent as much time together as they could, around his job and the store. Jesse got up early the next morning and met her for a quick run, then they went back to her place for a shower together before work. Mel rewarded him for his efforts by getting down on her knees while she was in there.

They did a lot of texting and a few late-night phone conversations.

Mel was getting to know him better and she couldn't believe she'd had such an awful opinion of him when they first met.

~

On Sunday Ellie, as promised, relieved Mel of her shift. She and Jesse drove to Houghton Bay so that Scrubber could run around off her leash. She was a very well-behaved dog, a fact Jesse was proud of. He'd trained her as a puppy and put in a lot of time with her.

They set up a blanket on the beach, and Jesse carried the chilly bin down, while Mel took the picnic basket. Jesse even had a yellow and white striped umbrella and it was a bit cute and romance movie-ish, Mel thought.

The water was still a bit cold. She needed to warm up first so she stripped down to her bikini and got settled with her book in the sun while Jesse threw sticks for Scrubber.

She was reading the newest Jodi Picoult but kept getting distracted by Jesse paddling in the water. He really was beautiful, she thought.

There was only a handful of people on the beach, mostly families. Mel watched Jesse as he held Scrubber when a young girl asked to pat her. He was good with kids and she wondered what he'd been like with Tama as a baby.

Mel liked kids, but she preferred them as they got bigger. She'd loved Fern's boys, and enjoyed cuddling them as infants, but she was really more into them as they got old enough to have conversations and do stuff with.

When Jesse came back and lay beside her, she asked him to tell her about Tama.

He told her about how much he'd loved giving him a bottle at night and bathing him when he got home from work. How he always said 'panana' instead of 'banana'.

"Do you want kids?" he asked her.

"Yeah, one day."

"How old are you anyway?"

"Twenty-eight."

Jesse grinned. "Ohh, I'm dating an older woman, that's hot."

"Oh hardly." Mel poked out her tongue.

"Anyway, if I wanted a toy boy, I'd date Skiddy." They both laughed.

"He is so in love with Ellie, he's a bloody liability at work these days, mooning over her." He looked a bit sheepish. "Still, I'm not much better, to be fair."

Mel laughed and Jesse leant over and kissed her belly button.

"Have I mentioned you look smokin' hot in that bikini?"

They swam, ate their picnic lunch, drank iced tea and lay in the sun reading and talking. Scrubber dug a hole that sprayed them in sand so they went back into the water to wash it off before they packed up for the day.

"Want to get a quick dinner and maybe come back to mine tonight?"

Mel looked down at her cut-off denim shorts and jandals.

"Shall we get a pizza and go back to yours to eat?"

"Yeah, sounds good. Saves me dropping Scrubber off first too. I'll ring Mere and see if she wants me to pick something up for them as well."

Mel realised she was going to meet Jesse's older sister and her husband Glen. She pulled down the visor and checked to see how bad she looked while Jesse talked. Her hair was a tangled mess so she finger-combed it and put it up in a messy bun, then fished around in her bag for a lip gloss.

Jesse had hung up and was watching her.

"I'm a wreck," Mel told him. "Your sister will think I was raised by wolves. Although, to be fair, that's fairly accurate in part."

"She's gonna love you," he said warmly, starting the car. "And remember, she's comparing you to Reia, so you've won already, babe."

~

Mere was lovely. She was a solid lady with warm eyes and the same full lips and wavy brown hair as Jesse. She was a registered nurse and her husband Glen was a mechanic. He was a huge guy, at least six foot five, and covered in tattoos with a full ginger beard and freckles. Mel wondered what their kids would look like if they had any.

They had been doing yard work all day and the pizza was a welcome reprieve from cooking, so the four of them sat out on the deck with a beer each and ate straight from the box. Scrubber ran around the big backyard chasing the sprinkler spray that was watering the vegetable garden, until Mere threw her a pizza crust.

"Don't feed her scraps. She'll get fat," Jesse growled.

"Oh, shut up, that's why she loves me." Mere slid a piece of pepperoni down the side of the chair to the dog's willing mouth.

"She loves everyone," Jesse grumbled. "Dogs don't eat till after we finish. She knows that."

Mere simply shrugged.

"So, Mel, it's nice to finally meet you. We've been hearing nothing but talk of you since July."

Mel looked at Jesse in surprise. "Is that right?"

Jesse stood up and started clearing the empty boxes to take inside, slapping his sister on the arm as he went past. Mere laughed. She had the same laugh as Jesse.

"Get me another beer while you're up will you, Jess?"

"And me," Glen and Mel called after him.

"At your service," Jesse said sarcastically as he went through the ranch slider.

The cicadas were singing and there was a light breeze. They sat in the sun talking and sipping their beers until the mozzies started to bite and they called it a night.

It had been a perfect day, Mel thought, as they got into Jesse's big king-sized bed and he pulled her towards him.

"Come here, my little cougar," he said with a laugh.

Chapter twenty-three

*"She hardly knew how to suppose that she could
be an object of admiration to so great a man."*

Pride and Prejudice, Jane Austen

Jesse made scrambled eggs and buttered sourdough toast for breakfast the next morning. They sat in the sun outside and watched Scrubber rolling on the grass. Mere and Glen had left for work before they'd woken up. Mel stretched contentedly. She could hear a tūī singing nearby, its distinctive warble loud in the quiet that surrounded them.

"It's lovely out here. It's so peaceful."

Mere and Glen's house was in Wilton, nestled in the bush.

"Yeah, I love it," Jesse agreed. "You want to go for a bush walk?"

"Can we take Scrubber?"

"As long as we keep her on a lead. Wanna go for a

walk, Scrubber?"

The dog perked her ears up and trotted over, hearing her name. She gave Mel a friendly sniff so Mel patted her head, rubbing her ear. Jesse collected up their empty plates and she followed him back inside and into the bedroom.

"I've only got yesterday's clothes."

He opened a draw and pulled out a T-shirt. "Here, borrow one of mine. Shower's through there."

Mel held the shirt to her nose and sniffed it as she closed the bathroom door behind her. It smelt of lavender washing powder but she was sure underneath there was a faint hint of Jesse as well.

~

Being a Monday morning they pretty much had the whole of the Ōtari-Wilton's Bush walk to themselves. Mel had never been there before and now wondered why — it was beautiful. So close to the city but you felt like you were miles away.

When they'd finished walking they went back to Jesse's and made sandwiches for lunch, then lounged around in the sun. It was a warm day and Mel felt lazy and content, not wanting to expend too much more energy.

Mel told Jesse about the time she'd spent in Rarotonga as a child. She and Fern had had a ball running wild with the local kids, swimming and exploring. None of the adults had worried too much about them; it was idyllic.

Jesse's upbringing had been similar, he said. Jumping off

bridges into the river, paddling round trying to catch eels. The older kids had kept an eye on the younger kids. Kids now didn't have as much freedom in that way.

"No mobile phones for us back then," Mel sighed.

"We didn't have shopping malls either. Or Xbox. I'd like my kids to grow up like I did, but that's probably unrealistic."

"When I think about it, Fern's actually not doing a bad job with Blade and Flint in that way. They're outside in the garden a lot, digging holes and making a mess. She doesn't like them to watch a lot of TV. They love to go on my iPad and watch cartoons, but that's because they don't have one themselves. I guess Marion and Geoff have made an impact on us in that way.

~

"Where are you going for Christmas?" Jesse asked her later as they lay in bed.

"My parents' house. They live in the Hutt. It'll be a mismatch of tofurkey and pavlova and edible flowers in salads,"' she told him. "We never really did Christmas when we were kids. Just another day really. Summer solstice was more my parents' style, but it's lovely now the boys are here and they're at a good age for the whole Santa thing."

"Did you really never have stockings?"

"Nope. Marion and Geoff thought it was wrong to encourage the lie. We didn't have the tooth fairy or the Easter bunny either. I was always so jealous of kids who got a stocking.

All the books I read as a kid had Christmas morning with the opening of a stocking full of oranges, chocolates, toys and treats. I mean, we did presents, sort of. We exchanged home-made things. Bookmarks, fudge, knitted hats and stuff. I guess I wanted a cheap plastic toy that would break in five minutes."

"Aww, poor little hippie girl." Jesse kissed her fingers.

"It wasn't all bad. We went to heaps of festivals and they were always fun. Fern and I got kittens one year. That was super exciting. I guess you want what you didn't have as kids. And probably why Fern and I stopped being vegan once we left home, much to Marion's disgust."

"Are they still vegan?"

"Mostly they're vegetarian since they eat eggs now, although I swear Geoff sneaks off now and then and has a burger," Mel laughed. "Dad's always been a peacekeeper and he'll do anything for Mum. As evidenced by the sculpture of cringe." She did a mock shiver.

"Although, I do see that appeal of the artistic process itself," she whispered into his neck as she ran her hands down into his boxers. "Perhaps I could do a little bit of moulding and kneading and see what happens?" Jesse laughed, but it quickly turned into a groan as Mel slid down his body.

"I'm so glad you stopped being a vegetarian," he moaned, making Mel crack up and completely lose her concentration.

~

Tuesday came. It was only three days until Christmas but Mel felt fantastic after two days off and she was full of Christmas cheer as she opened the shop. She'd made more gingerbread people and cheese muffins and she lit a pine-scented candle Marion had made for her. The shop smelt heavenly and she was sitting, sipping her turmeric latte and making more lists for the party when Olive arrived.

"Good morning, don't you look nice," Mel told her. Olive was wearing a lovely peach-coloured blouse with ruffled sleeves. She smiled shyly at the compliment.

"Thanks, Mel. A little early Christmas gift to myself. I watch you and Ellie and I've realised I need to spruce myself up a bit. Too long working with oldies, I think."

"Why did you get into elderly care?" Mel asked.

"My mum went into a home with Alzheimer's," Olive said. "I spent so much time there, that after she passed, they asked if I'd be interested in staying on in a paid role. But I think maybe I need to get out and be around people more my age. That's why I enjoy it so much here."

"Are you coming to the Christmas party?" Mel asked her.

"Yes, I'm looking forward to it. It's a lovely gesture."

The bell rang, and Colin walked in, smiling at them both, and making Olive blush.

"Ladies, isn't it a beautiful morning? I thought I'd amble over and trouble you for a pot of tea. My first client cancelled last minute. Terribly rude, but nevertheless, I shan't complain."

"Indeed," Mel said. "Olive, tea for you too?"

"Yes, please, Mel, and a little ginger person too, if I may."

"How politically correct of you, Melody," Colin chuckled drily. "Perhaps," he said to Olive, "if it's not an imposition, I could join you to partake of our tea?"

"Why, yes, of course," Olive told him, looking rather pleased.

Mel stifled a laugh, and went to make their tea. It was like something from a very dull period drama, she thought.

"I don't suppose you've come to your senses about the Shakespeare festival?" Colin asked Mel as she set down the cups on the small table between them.

"Ah, no. Sorry, Colin, but as I said, I can't spare the time."

Colin turned to Olive. "Are you, perchance, a fan of the bard?" he asked, and Mel took her chance to leave.

Ellie had left her a note to say they had a group of twelve booked in for Wednesday night for a book club Christmas do and that she'd be in a little earlier to help Mel get ready and do party prep. Underneath she'd written:

PS Aaron came in on Sunday to buy his mum another book, and gave me flowers! Help!! I may have to tell him I'm a lesbian!

Mel really doubted that would put him off.

Jesse had planned for them to have dinner down on the waterfront that night since they had the last of the wine and cheese evenings for the year on Wednesday and the party Thursday. Jesse had shut down and closed up the building site last Friday and he, Mere and Glen were heading off to his parents' place on Christmas Eve after Mere's last shift.

They often had a hāngī for dinner, he'd told her, but not this year since his dad wasn't going to make it back. They were hoping to do a spit instead, so Glen and Jesse were planning to get a hunt in when they got there and shoot a pig. It was always a big gathering, with all the family and lots of extras who tagged along. Mel thought it sounded fantastic and she was a little envious.

The city was buzzing in the lead-up to Christmas, even on a Tuesday, although many of the students had left to go home by now and Mel knew it would be quieter over the summer because of that. After they'd eaten, she and Jesse held hands and strolled, enjoying the balmy weather. Wellington wasn't known for its great climate and probably because of this, the locals appreciated it more and they were out in droves.

"You want to get a cocktail before we head home?" Jesse asked.

"Sure."

They found a bar and pushed their way through a group of people celebrating Christmas drinks. Mel ordered while Jesse went off to find a table. As she carried their drinks over she happened to glance over and saw Claire sitting near the window. Of course she got a prime table, Mel thought. She'd probably have demanded one, knowing Claire. She was positive Claire had seen her but was studiously ignoring that she had, which suited Mel fine.

"Just going to have a wee," she told Jesse, rather than sitting down. "Back in a sec."

The corridor to the bathrooms was quiet and Mel was humming to herself when suddenly someone came barrelling out of the men's toilets and shoved past her.

"Oh, sor—" she started, when the man turned and she realised it was Nate.

He rubbed at his nose and sniffed loudly, his eyes wild.

He looked at her blankly for a few seconds and then his brow furrowed and his eyes narrowed in recognition.

"You fucking bitch," he sneered, pushing her shoulder and pinning her against the wall.

Taken by surprise, Mel didn't know what to say.

"What bloody stories have you been telling Claire?"

Mel felt her blood boil.

"Nothing that wasn't true. You were trying to get me to sleep with you and all the while you had a girlfriend. I didn't even get to tell her about Jesse's sister Nia and how you planted drugs on her."

Nate looked thunderous, and Mel really wished that he wasn't her landlord.

"So what? I knew she wouldn't get into that much shit, and even if she did ..."

There was a gasp behind them and they turned to see Claire who, judging by the shocked look on her face, had obviously overheard.

"Nate? What's going on?"

Nate looked shifty. And nervous. Claire was looking between the two of them, her face furrowed in confusion.

At that moment Jesse appeared behind Claire and strode over to Nate who still had Mel up against the wall. Roughly he pulled him away and without a word punched him hard in the face. Blood spurted from his nose and dripped onto his fancy suit, staining the pristine white shirt.

Claire's hand shot up to cover her mouth in horror.

"My nose!" Nate spluttered. But it came out more like "*By dose!*"

"Why do you always have to be the centre of everything, you little slut?" Claire said furiously to Mel, and without looking at Nate, turned and stormed away down the corridor. He followed her wordlessly, holding his hand up to his dripping face.

Mel eyed Jesse, who was still looking furious but also kind of pleased with himself.

"God, that felt good. I've wanted to punch that prick for years. Are you okay?"

"I'm fine. A bit shaken up, I guess, but I'm okay."

He gave her a long hug. "What do you think Claire will do now?"

"Probably pretend it didn't happen. Her big society wedding will be too important, I reckon. Did you see how coked up he looked though?"

"Yeah, I noticed. Do you want to leave?"

"No, I want to have a wee and drink my cocktail."

"What were you doing out there anyway, if you weren't going to the toilet?" Mel asked when she got back to the table.

"I saw Claire watching you, then get up and follow you out. Something just seemed a bit off about it."

"I wonder what she would have said to me if Nate hadn't been there."

Jesse shrugged. "Maybe she knew Nate was out there and thought he might hit on you again. She probably suspected you were telling the truth about that. What reason would you have to lie?"

Mel stirred the ice around in her glass. "You think she wanted to catch him out?"

"Maybe, I guess we'll never know."

"She heard what I said though and he didn't deny it.

Though he'll probably try to later."

"I'd guess it's not the first time he's done something like that. He's a bloody scumbag. And the drug use is going to be pretty hard to hide, unless she already knows about that."

Jesse shifted forward in his seat. "You make sure you call me if he hassles you again."

~

They finished their drinks and wandered back along the waterfront, passing a group of young people listening to music on a Bluetooth speaker near the train station and walked up the hill to Mel's place. Jesse was carrying their leftovers from dinner in a cardboard box and had his other arm comfortably around Mel. They were making the most of their time together before he left to go home for the Christmas break. He'd be coming back on New Year's Eve and they were discussing what they might do.

Kevin, looking shaggier and more grizzled than ever, passed them coming down the hill and gave them a nod.

"Hey, mate," Jesse called to him, "you hungry?"

Kevin gratefully took the food from them with a mumbled thanks. Jesse stood and watched as he continued on his way, a puzzled and slightly amused look on his face. He turned to Mel.

"Are those my socks he's wearing?"

Mel looked at Kevin's legs. His trousers were too short for him and the black and pink polka dot socks were clearly visible underneath.

"Um, yeah, I might have given them to him," Mel said sheepishly.

"They're my lucky socks. I wondered where they'd got to."

"What's so lucky about them?"

He grinned and put his arm around her again. "Well, I got you, didn't I?"

Chapter twenty-four

"Her heart did whisper that he had done it for her."

Pride and Prejudice, Jane Austen

Mel left Jesse showering while she went to open up the shop the next morning. She flicked on the Christmas music, went into the kitchen and took down the plastic container of brandy snaps she'd made the day before. It had been fun making Christmas treats and a change from her usual baking.

Jesse came thundering down the stairs a few minutes later and she was glad he'd fixed the railing, sure it would have torn right off if he hadn't.

He gave her a quick kiss, the keys to his truck in his hand.

"Back later, babe, you want me to pick anything up?"

"No, I should be good. I'll text you if I think of anything."

She watched as he headed out the door, realising she was really going to miss him when he left the next day.

Within a few moments he was back, a scowl plastered on his face.

"Bloody hell. Someone's slashed my tyres overnight."

"Are you sure? It's not just a flat?"

"Nope, all of them have been done." He scrolled through the contacts on his phone.

"Lucky I've got a friend who's a towie. Hopefully he won't be too busy."

"Probably some kids mucking about," Mel said. "Though it seems pretty extreme and it's usually pretty quiet around here at night."

Jesse was thoughtful. "Yeah, that's true. Maybe someone's got it in for me. Fuck it," he sighed. "Still, at least two of them were a bit bald, I suppose."

"You can claim insurance if you make a police report, can't you?"

Mel walked over and looked out the front window, wondering if Nate's car would be parked across the road. She saw Claire quickly moving away from where she was standing, visible in her own store frontage. Would she do something like that, Mel wondered? She hated any cars parked on the road and Jesse's muddy old ute would be top of her hate list. Still, it seemed over the top, unless it was to get back at her somehow?

She checked her emails and sent out a Christmas message

to their customers, informing them of their opening days over the holiday season. She could hear Jesse talking on the phone in the background. He wandered over to her and kissed the back of her neck.

"Dan's gonna be here in about twenty."

"Want a coffee?"

"I'd marry you for one," he said and then looked embarrassed. They both laughed awkwardly.

"No need to buy the cow, I'm giving you the milk for free," Mel joked to lighten the tension, reaching into the fridge for a bottle.

"Do you want to get married?" he asked, then quickly added, "I don't mean *now*. That wasn't a proposal. But ever?"

Mel thought about it for a bit while she heated the milk.

"Maybe, I dunno. It's not really something I'm hung up on though. Marion and Geoff never got married and I never dreamed of the whole church and white dress thing as a kid. Do you?"

He shrugged. "I guess."

She handed him his coffee. "Well, I'll tell you what, if I decide I do, you'll be the first to know." They both grinned and sat, listening to 'Snoopy's Christmas' and drinking their coffees.

"I hate this fucking song," Jesse announced, as Ellie arrived in the door, bell jingling and her arms full of bags.

"Ergh, I hate this song," she said, making Mel and Jesse laugh.

The last day in the store was busy, and the wine and cheese night went well. They didn't finish until almost eleven. Jesse had come and helped them with dishes and mopped the floor.

Mel lay in his bed that night trying to think of anything they might have missed for their party. Scrubber snored lightly next to them in her bed on the floor. Outside Mel could hear a morepork calling. She rechecked her alarm and stuck one foot out the edge of the duvet. Jesse mumbled something in his sleep and turned towards her and she looked at his face in the moonlight and smiled.

~

When they got back to her place the next morning, Mel was horrified to find the word 'SLUT' spray-painted on her display window in bright-red paint. She got out of the ute slowly as she took it in.

"Oh my God, what the hell?" Scrubber whined on the back of the ute and Mel scratched her ear distractedly. "Who the fuck? Bloody hell. I do not need to deal with this today."

Jesse inspected the graffiti. "Don't stress, babe, it's only on the glass and it's bound to scrape off and clean up with a bit of turps. I'll go next door and see if I can find some bits to use."

He gave her a kiss, and rubbed his hand up and down her back gently. "You go do your stuff, I'll sort it."

Mel went into the bookstore, feeling a bit off balance from

it all, and told herself to concentrate on the things they needed to do for that night. She tried not to dwell too much but hadn't Claire called her a slut at the bar? Was she out to pay back Mel for getting involved in her relationship with Nate? Was she trying to shoot the messenger? Christ, she hoped Claire didn't own a gun.

The doorbell jangled and Mel jumped. Marion came in, looking worried.

"Melly, love, what on earth happened with your window?" Outside, Jesse had scraped most of the word off. Mel made a drinking motion to him to see if he wanted coffee and he gave her a vigorous nod.

"Vandals, I guess," Mel told her. "What are you doing here so early?"

"I'm on my way to Fern's. The boys and I are making cookies to leave for Santa, but I wanted to drop these off first." She handed over a parcel and Mel curiously unwrapped the brown paper.

"Cheeses. I made them myself," Marion declared. "For tonight. They're soy based." Jesse came in and poured himself a water from the tap.

"What are all the brown bits?" Mel asked as she peered at the two slightly greyish lumps. "Poppy seeds?"

"Chia seeds," Marion said. "They're fabulous things. You can put them in anything. They're a good source of omega-3 and fibre too."

"Okay, well ... thanks," Mel said slowly. "They look ...

interesting."

"Oh, darling, your sculpture's back to front again," Marion declared, heading towards the shelf where it had been tucked as discreetly as possible into the corner.

"You need to have it on full display at the party for any prospective buyers to see, especially while I'm there to discuss it with them. Perhaps we could put it on the counter?" She reached for the offending item. Mel blanched.

"Here, let me," Jesse said suddenly, reaching up for the piece and moving it towards the front counter. Then he tripped, quite dramatically over his foot, and the sculpture went flying. It smashed into several large chunks on the wood floor.

"Whoops, I'm so sorry," he said earnestly to Marion. "I'm so clumsy. I feel terrible."

"No, no, it's fine," Marion assured him. "I'm sure it was an accident." Mel wasn't so sure. She looked at Jesse as Marion bent over to pick up one of the larger shards and he gave her a wink. I could fall in love with him, Mel thought.

"I'll pay for it of course," he told her mother.

"No, nonsense, you don't need to do that," she insisted. "I can always do another one sometime."

Mel hoped she would move on to a new phase before then.

"Anyway, I must go, the kids have been up since six and Fern will be pulling her hair out." She gave Mel a kiss. "I'll see you tonight," she told her. She kissed Jesse too. "Drive safe, and a merry holidays to you and your family," she said warmly.

After she'd left, Mel put her arms around Jesse's waist, leant up and kissed him gently. "My hero," she said, making him laugh. "Want some breakfast?"

"Sure." He cut off a piece of Marion's cheese wedge and put it in his mouth while Mel fished out some bread to toast, then quickly spat it out into his hand.

"Bloody hell," he muttered. Mel looked over at him.

"Is it as bad as it looks?" she asked, trying a small piece herself. It was worse, she decided.

"Good Lord. I can't put that out on the table tonight, and she's bound to notice and ask where it is."

"Tell her Scrubber got into it and ate it," Jesse suggested.

"I'm a terrible liar though."

"Well, then we'll give it to her. That way it's not really a lie." He took the offending package out and opened it on the bed of the truck. Mel could hear his booming laugh and he came back in, still grinning.

"She wouldn't touch it," he said with another laugh. "Normally she eats anything. Sorry."

~

After breakfast Jesse finished cleaning the window and then got a text from Glen to say they were ready to go.

Mel felt a bit emotional as they said their goodbyes.

"Oh, I nearly forgot your present," she said, handing him the wrapped book. "There's something for Scrubber too."

"Can I open it now?" he asked.

"Sure."

She'd thrown in a new pair of 'lucky' socks for him — these ones had watermelons on them — and he grinned. He looked at the book, and gave her a funny look. "Trying to get rid of me?"

"No. Not at all. Quite the opposite in fact," she said quietly. "I'm going to miss you."

"Me too," he said, kissing her again. "Thanks. Yours is under the tree, but wait till tomorrow to open it, okay?"

They kissed again, until Jesse's phone dinged twice.

"I'll see you New Year's Eve."

"Okay, but text me when you get there."

He blew her a kiss out the window as he drove off and Mel went to find the vacuum cleaner in case there were still bits of sculpture they'd missed with the broom.

Chapter twenty-five

"Follies and nonsense, whims and inconsistencies, do divert me, I own, and I laugh at them whenever I can."

Pride and Prejudice, Jane Austen

Mel's morning turned quickly into lunchtime, and she was getting a bit stressed. She managed to burn one lot of the Christmas mince pies, and her hand as she got them out. The smoke had set off her detector and she was frantically waving a tea towel at it when Ellie arrived, looking flustered too.

"I've fucked up the champagne order," she told Mel. "I'm such an idiot. Somehow I managed to have it sent to Mum and Dad's place instead of here, and they already left for Welly half an hour ago. Brandon rang to tell me it was there, and no one else at the winery is headed this way."

"Shit. What are we going to do? Have we got anything left in the budget to get some at the bottle store?" Mel asked, throwing the burnt pies out the back door for the birds.

"Nope, and we'd have to pay retail which means getting something crappy. I'd rather not serve shit when we're trying to build up our reputation for having good wine, you know?"

Mel agreed.

"What have we got here? Anything? Or do we serve a white or something?"

"I'll go see what we've got," Ellie said glumly. "Sorry, Mel, I'm an idiot."

"Nah, shit happens," Mel said, trying not to feel too frustrated.

She was putting a new batch of pies in the oven when Ellie came back, a bottle under her arm.

"What does this stuff taste like?" she asked hopefully. She was carrying one of Geoff's elderflower wines.

"No idea, but I imagine it's not great."

"Well, there are thirteen bottles there, so I'm opening one to try," Ellie announced. "It's either this or a mix of rosé and Sauvignon Blancs."

She poured a chug into a nearby coffee cup and took a sip. Then another.

"Shit, that's actually bloody nice," she told Mel with a grin. "Seriously."

She poured another cup and Mel took a tentative sip. "Wow."

"Go, Geoff."

Ellie went back to the store cupboard to fetch the bottles

and load them into the wine fridge, while Mel took out the thankfully perfectly done pies.

The party was from five to seven but Ellie's parents came a little earlier to see the shop.

Grahame was a handsome man, quite the silver fox, Mel thought as she always did whenever she met him. She was glad she hadn't known Ellie in high school. She'd have had a terrible crush on him. He gave her a big hug and so did Julia. She was like Ellie, tiny and blonde.

"We're so proud of you girls," she told them. "You've done an amazing job with this place." She admired Mel's copy of George's book under the glass counter. "I love that book," she told her. They talked for a bit about George, and Ellie came in with a tray of champagne flutes.

"Let's have a toast, shall we?" She reached into the fridge for a bottle.

They all clinked glasses. "To the girls," Grahame toasted.

"And to George," Mel said.

"Merry Christmas," Julia added.

They sipped their bubbles.

"Hmmm, that's very good," Grahame said to Ellie. "Whose winery is it from?" As if he'd been summoned, Geoff popped his head in the door with a cheery hello. Ellie set about pouring more bubbles as the parents did their hellos, and Ellie's parents oohed and ahhed over Fern and her now well-developed bump.

The boys were supposed to be home with Chase, so Fern gave Mel an apologetic grimace as they came in behind her.

"I'm so sorry. Bloody Chase decided to leave a day early for his parents' place. A friend of mine is coming to get them soon to take them to see the Christmas lights out at Miramar, so they won't be here long."

"It's fine, really." Mel gave both boys a hug and a kiss. "Do you two want a juice each?"

"Can we have it in a fancy glass?" Blade asked.

"No," Fern told them, "and don't touch anything. Santa is watching, remember?"

Both boys looked around nervously and kept their hands firmly by their sides.

"I do see the merits of this whole Santa thing now," Marion said with a laugh.

"Geoff, you and I must talk," Grahame told him. "This wine is fantastic. I'd love to stock it at the vineyard. Perhaps get you on an exclusive contract before anyone else gets wind of it." He and Geoff wandered down to one of the back tables and sat, deep in conversation. Mel took them down a plate of cheese and crackers. Geoff gave her a grateful smile, looking pleased and overwhelmed by Grahame's enthusiasm.

Slowly, people arrived. The wine flowed and the food was eaten. Everyone was in great spirits.

Fern left early. Her friend had brought the kids back and offered to drop them all home. It wasn't any fun, Fern told Mel, being the sober one at a party. The boys were so excited, they'd be up at sparrow's fart the next morning. They arranged for Fern to pick Mel up the next day to head to their parents for lunch.

Albert had brought them a lovely posy of flowers from his garden and was thrilled when Mel and Ellie gave him a braided bookmark, courtesy of Marion.

Mel gave one to Olive too when she saw her.

"Mr Exeter and I are going to attend the Shakespeare festival together," Olive said blushing furiously. "We're going to fly down and spend the night. Separate rooms, of course." They looked over at Colin, who was talking earnestly to Julia. Mel watched as Julia chugged down her drink and quickly excuse herself to get more.

"He's very intriguing," Olive went on. "Forthright and strong with his convictions. We have a lot in common regarding books." She blushed again. "Anyway, I heard Claire was engaged, but she broke it off. Colin told me she threw a bag of his things out on the street last night after closing."

Good for her, thought Mel, looking over at the boutique and feeling a little guilty that they hadn't invited her over. Then she thought of the window, and quickly changed her mind.

Colin came over and lay his hand possessively on the small of Olive's back.

"You ladies look deep in conversation. Are you telling Miss Hawkins about our planned weekend excursion?"

"Yes, I'm sure you'll both have a fabulous time," Mel said warmly. "Christchurch is a great city too."

"Well, you had your chance," Colin told her in a rather grave tone, and Mel laughed.

"I suppose I did," she agreed. "Never mind. You'll have to tell us all about it when you get back."

"Perhaps you and Jesse could meet us for a meal sometime?" Olive suggested.

"Hmm, well, perhaps," Mel said noncommittally. She couldn't think of anything worse, she thought, except maybe a double date with Claire and Nate. No offence to Olive, who had become something of a friend.

Eventually the party faded out, until only Mel, Ellie and her parents were left to clean up the last few things.

"What time are you heading off in the morning?" Mel asked.

"We're actually going to head back tonight," Julia told her. "Grahame's only had one drink and he hates sleeping at Ellie's with all the city noise." Mel looked at her watch. It was almost eight.

"Go, go," she told them. "It's getting late. I can do all this."

"Are you sure?" Ellie asked hopefully.

"Absolutely."

They all hugged goodbye.

"I'll see you on New Year's Eve," Ellie said, "but we'll talk tomorrow?"

"Love you," Mel called as she waved them off.

She shut the door to the store and locked it, then leant against it with a contented sigh.

Chapter twenty-six

*"I sincerely hope your Christmas ... may abound
in the gaieties which the season generally brings."*

Pride and Prejudice, Jane Austen

Having never really been a big Christmas person, Mel slept in the next morning and it was after nine by the time she got up, throwing on a robe over her pyjamas.

She made tea and popped bread into the toaster, picking up her phone to message Jesse a Merry Christmas. On cue it dinged with a message from him and she grinned as she read it:

Dont forget to check under the tree xx

She ran downstairs, almost as excited as a child, but hoping he hadn't got her anything too extravagant, as she'd only given him the book. Peering under the tree she couldn't see anything at first and then she noticed it, tucked in the back.

A bright red and green Christmas stocking, embroidered with a tubby-looking Santa Claus.

Mel may have squealed.

Sitting on the top was an orange and a small bar of Whittaker's chocolate. Beneath that was a large red and white striped candy cane. The first package she took out had a sticky label reading 'TO MEL FROM SANTA', and when she ripped it open she found a garish, plastic pink and purple necklace, which she put on straight away.

Two more parcels followed. One was a tub of glow-in-the-dark slime and the other a cute cuddly teddy bear. He was wearing a pair of shorts and a builder's tool belt, which made Mel grin. She reached for her phone.

~

After she'd spoken to Jesse, far longer than she'd intended, she jumped into the shower and dressed. Fern had texted to say the boys were overexcited and they'd be around a bit earlier than planned. Christmas at her parents was never a big deal, so she didn't need to get dressed up, and she'd come back down to the shop in shorts and a T-shirt when she noticed Kevin knocking tentatively on the window.

She unlocked the door and stepped out.

"Sorry to interrupt your morning but I wanted to give you this." He held something out to her in his hand. "I wanted to say thank you for your kindness."

Mel took it from him and examined the object. It was a

pīwakawaka, or fantail, intricately carved from a piece of wood.

"Did you make this?" she asked in wonder.

He nodded. "It's not much," he said humbly. "I like to keep my hand in. I'm a carpenter by trade, though that seems like a lifetime ago now."

"Kevin, it's absolutely beautiful. I'm waiting for my sister to pick me up. Can I get you a coffee?"

"I don't want to be any bother."

"It's not, not at all. Come in."

Before they could head back inside, Fern pulled up. The back door of the car opened and Flint and Blade spilled out.

"Aunty Mel, Aunty Mel, where are our presents?" Flint yelled.

Mel pretended to look surprised. "Is it Christmas? I forgot."

Flint wasn't fooled though. "No, you didn't, I saw them under the tree yesterday. There was a big box with my name on it."

"He peeked," Blade accused. "I saw him." He threw his arms around Mel in a fierce hug.

"Did not. I wanted to hug Aunty Mel first," Flint yelled, wrapping his arms around Mel's legs. They were obviously super hyped up.

She noticed Kevin had started to amble away and called after him. "Where are you going to spend the day?"

Turning back he shrugged. "Probably head down the waterfront. I think they're doing a meal down at the church later. That'll be nice."

To Mel's surprise it was Fern who spoke. "That doesn't sound like much fun. Why don't you come with us to Mum and Dad's?"

Mel had been planning to suggest the same.

"I couldn't do that." Kevin said, but he'd stopped walking for the moment.

"Of course you can. We don't have a traditional Christmas Day and Marion and Geoff always invite extras. They'd love to have you. Seriously."

He looked down at his clothes, seeming embarrassed. "I couldn't."

"We insist," Mel told him. "Mum and Dad have a fantastic outdoor bath, if that would make you feel better. I can squash in the back with the boys, you sit up front with Fern."

"A bath *would* be lovely," Kevin said longingly.

"Then it's settled," Fern said firmly. "Have you got everything, Mel?"

"I'll pop in and get the presents and lock up. And make Kevin a coffee for the trip. Oh, Kevin, this is Fern by the way, my sister."

She made coffees, grabbed the presents she'd boxed up earlier and squeezed into the back between Flint and Blade who told her all about their Santa stockings on the way.

~

Geoff was first to greet them when they arrived, almost being bowled over by the boys first.

"Can we have our presents?" Flint asked, and Blade looked equally keen.

"Go and have a look under the tree," Geoff chuckled, holding out a hand to Kevin and introducing himself.

"Geoff, Kevin would love to try out the outdoor bath," Mel told him, and the two of them went off around the back of the house, Geoff chatting amiably. He was a laid-back man and good at putting people at ease. Mel was sure he'd come up with some clean clothes Kevin could wear as well, and wouldn't make a big deal about it so Kevin would feel comfortable accepting them.

Marion was handing presents to the boys and Mel dumped her box of goodies on the coffee table. She went over and kissed her mother on the cheek.

"Merry Christmas, Marion, and happy solstice too."

"We've been too busy to celebrate this year," Marion said, kissing her back and then Fern too, "so this is a double celebration. Who was that you had with you?"

"That's Kevin," Mel told her. "He didn't have anywhere to go so we persuaded him to come with us. Have you got any extras coming for lunch?"

"No, not this year, so it will be nice to have a new face. It's a pity your young man's not here, Mel. Chase too," she added politely, even though Mel was pretty sure she didn't think much of him.

"Well, I'm glad Chase isn't here," Fern said bitterly, dropping down onto the sofa. She rubbed her belly and sighed deeply. Mel suspected that was where she would stay for the rest of the day, using her pregnancy as an excuse to get out of doing anything related to cooking or cleaning up.

"Have things not been going well, love?" Marion asked. She handed Fern a wine glass filled with a bubbly, green-tinged liquid.

"Mum, you know I can't drink."

"It's sparkling kiwifruit juice. Geoff made it specially."

Fern took a sip and grimaced. "It's okay, but, man, I miss alcohol. I can't wait for this kid to be born."

"He's going to be our brother." Flint looked up from playing with a pile of cars Marion and Geoff had given the boys. Blade was patiently assembling a series of wooden pieces that made up a car ramp that Marion had made them. It was actually quite impressive.

"Hurry up, Blade," Flint whined.

"He's going to be called Steel," Blade added. "Wait, Flint, it's not done yet."

"Here, Flint, open this one from me." Mel handed over a parcel to distract him.

"Do you think perhaps you could use some counselling?" Marion was asking Fern, looking concerned. "I know a lady who is brilliant."

"No, I doubt Chase would go for that. Anyway, I think we already know it's not going to work out. He says he wants to be involved with the baby, so that's cool, I guess." She shrugged and took another sip of her drink.

"Well, I'm sorry anyway, sweetheart. You know Geoff and I will do whatever we can to help. Perhaps the boys could stay with us for a bit to give you a break?"

"Yeah, thanks, they'd love that."

"And we'd love to have them."

Mel left Fern sitting on the sofa and wandered into the kitchen with her mother.

"Can I do something?" she asked.

"You can whip the coconut cream for the ambrosia while I cut some carrot sticks. Move those seedlings off the bench onto the shelf over there," she replied as she rinsed a bunch of carrots, stalks on and fresh soil still clinging. Mel moved the plants, delicate little things growing in an old egg carton, onto a shelf, already crammed with art supplies and self-help books.

The kitchen was a mess of dishes. Marion was an untidy cook and Geoff the opposite. Usually he went along behind her tidying up. Before she dealt with whipping the cream, Mel ran water in the sink and started on the dishes, while her mother gave her a rundown on the latest caravan project and promised to show Mel later. Mel loved the caravans her parents refurbished. They both had a real talent for it. They stuck mostly to vintage style, usually nineteen seventies, but this latest one had a nautical theme.

Their first project had been the house truck they'd lived in when she and Fern were kids. Geoff had built them the best bunk beds ever, like something out of a fairy tale, and he'd made improvements for other travellers when they'd needed them, for extra cash.

Her father poked his head in the door, Kevin behind him, dressed in a pair of brown corduroy pants and a checked shirt. Mel had the feeling it might be the one she'd given Geoff for his birthday earlier in the year. Kevin had also washed his hair and had a shave and Mel was surprised to see he was a lot younger than she'd originally thought.

"Drinks?" Geoff asked.

Once they'd settled in the living room and Geoff had put his famous tofurkey roast into the oven, Mel showed everyone the wooden bird Kevin had carved for her. Her father turned it over, examining it carefully.

"Kevin, this is really something," he told him. "It's exceptional work."

"It's pretty rough. If I still had my tools I'd have done a much better job."

"Can you make me one?" Blade asked. "That's cool."

"Me too," Flint insisted, never to be outdone.

"Kevin was a cabinet-maker when he left school," Mel told them.

"I've always loved working with my hands. I could build pretty much anything, if I put my mind to it," he said proudly. "The company I worked for went out of business and there wasn't much work in the small town I grew up in. So, I moved away and did casual work on farms and orchards, but I got sick a few years ago and wasn't able to work. I've never been able to get things together after that."

He seemed embarrassed to have said so much and got down on the floor to help the boys put the batteries into the walkie-talkies and show them how to operate them.

"Let's take these outside," he told them, and the boys yelled with excitement and led the way into the garden.

"What a nice man," Fern sighed, obviously pleased that the boys weren't yelling in their faces any more.

Geoff looked thoughtful as he watched them go.

"I could really do with someone to help out around here," he said. "Especially if we're going to start producing the elderflower wine for Grahame."

"Well, it's going to be too busy to do that and the rebuilds." Marion turned to him. "Are you thinking Kevin? We could probably only offer him part-time hours to start with, but we've got a spare caravan he could live in so he wouldn't have to pay rent."

~

They ate way too much as usual and blobbed out for the afternoon while the boys played with their toys. Jesse phoned Mel again and she slipped outside onto the deck to talk to him. She could hear a lot of laughter and shouting in the background and someone was playing a guitar. It sounded fun.

Glen had cut his leg when he slipped on the zoom slide, they hadn't managed to catch a pig so had eaten roast chicken instead and a cousin had announced he was getting married, Jesse told her.

"I miss you though. You'll have to come up here with me next year."

"Miss you too."

Things were pretty good.

~

The boys got scratchy around seven as they'd been up early, so she and Fern helped tidy up and they packed children and presents into the car and hugged their parents goodbye.

Fern was going to bring the boys back out in a few days and she'd bring Kevin as well. He and Geoff had had a talk and come to an agreement and Kevin seemed in great spirits.

"Do you have somewhere to stay tonight?" Fern asked Kevin, "because you're welcome to sleep on our couch."

"Oh, I couldn't," Kevin said.

"Why?" Fern asked, genuinely perplexed. "It's Christmas, we have space, and if you can handle two loud early alarms," she nodded towards the sleepy boys in the back, "you're more than welcome. We'd be happy to have you."

"Thank you, Fern," Kevin said quietly, and Mel saw him wipe a tear from the corner of his eye.

~

At home, Mel changed into her pyjamas and made herself a
cup of tea. Then she climbed into bed with a book, her little
builder bear perched on the pillow beside her.

Chapter twenty-seven

*"My courage always rises with every
attempt to intimidate me."*
Pride and Prejudice, Jane Austen

Boxing Day in New Zealand meant sales and shopping for much of the population. The malls were always crazy busy. Pinot and Pūhā was closed so Mel texted Fern to see if she wanted to take the boys to the zoo with her. They arranged for Fern to pick her up after she'd fed the boys lunch.

Mel pottered around the shop, putting away all the cleaned platters and chopping boards and the glasses back onto the shelves. She sprayed some oven cleaner and left it, thinking it would be a good job for the next day. Then she gathered up the last of the wine bottles and took them out to the recycling bin.

Claire was coming out of her door across the road and Mel

thought about what Olive had said about her throwing Nate's belongings into the street. She really didn't want to be at war with Claire. It had been bad enough before with all her niggly complaints, but she could at least try and smooth things over.

"Claire," she called, crossing the road and giving a little wave, "can I have a word?" Claire gave her a haughty look. She was perfectly made up in a fifties-style dress, her hair in a chignon and lips red.

"What do you want now?"

"I wanted to check that you were okay. Olive mentioned that you and Nate had split up and I didn't want there to be any hard feelings between us after the other night."

Claire didn't answer but stared at Mel, her eyes narrowing. She looked tired, Mel thought.

"Anyway, I hope you had a nice day yesterday—"

"I most certainly did not," Claire spat out. "I had to tell my parents their dream wedding was no longer. I had to cancel our engagement party and it's all thanks to your interfering and gossip. Swanning around in front of him with your cleavage out and encouraging him, then spreading rumours about drugs. You've ruined everything. I hope you die," she yelled dramatically, then covered her mouth with her hand in horror and started to cry. Mel noticed she still had on the ring.

"Claire, look—"

"Oh, piss off!" Claire shouted. "You and Nate are welcome

to each other. Just go away."

She turned and stormed into her shop, slamming the red front door behind her.

Mel stared after her, a bit dumbfounded. Colin was watching her from down the road as he unlocked his door, she realised, a bit mortified.

"Right, well, that went well. Great job, Mel," she said out loud as she went back to her side of the street.

~

The zoo was really quiet as she had hoped, with only a handful of people wandering around. They spent ages watching the otters swimming and playing, and wandered around stopping anywhere the animals caught someone's attention.

"Kevin was gone when I got up," Fern said. "But he'd tidied up and he left me a bunch of flowers on the table." She laughed. "I think they were from the neighbours on my right."

"The old grumpy ones?" Mel asked.

"Yeah. She always complains that the boys are in the yard too much, being noisy."

"Do you think she'll notice?"

"Probably, but who cares. I thought it was lovely he bothered."

The sun bear was, as usual, Mel's favourite. They ate ice creams while they watched the red pandas eating and then Flint started to complain he was hot.

"I think he's tired," Fern said, which set him off wailing that he wasn't.

"Shall we go home and fill up the little pool?" she suggested. It was too small really for the boys now, but there wasn't room for anything much bigger on her little section. They left them slathered in sunscreen and with the hose going slowly and went inside for a drink, and to avoid the neighbour.

"Do you want to stay for dinner?" Fern asked, and Mel was going to say no, but Fern looked so hopeful. She didn't do well on her own, never had.

"Sure," Mel agreed. "What are we having?"

"I was going to make something easy. Mum gave me a heap of leftovers."

Mel had a look in the fridge. "Oh, shall we throw some feta into the roast veges and have a salad? Have you got basil?"

"Yeah, on the windowsill, but I doubt the boys will eat it."

"I'll do them some eggs and soldiers, shall I?" Mel suggested. She got busy pottering in the kitchen and it was a while before she realised how quiet Fern was.

"You okay, Silver?"

Fern smiled a little at the old nickname. "Yeah, maybe a bit down. I have such shit taste in men. I never find the good ones. And I've done nothing with my life, no job, no travel. Why is everything so easy for you?"

Mel tried hard not to be offended by that. Fern seemed to have the idea that everything just fell into Mel's lap in life. She envied Mel every job she got and for the money George had left her, conveniently forgetting that Mel had had to work hard at school and uni to get to that point. That she'd worked crap jobs on the way there. Fern had gone from school, to having Blade, gone on the DPB, and never left. She'd never tried having a job, even part time.

"You're only twenty-six," she said kindly. "You've got heaps of time left to do things, decide what you want to do. Maybe you should look at some online study?" She'd suggested that before, but Fern really wasn't interested.

"Maybe," Fern agreed. She called the boys in to eat.

"How old do you think Kevin is?" she asked Mel, as she helped Flint cut the top off his egg, and something about her tone made Mel stop and look at her sister twice.

~

The next morning, after a ridiculously early night, Mel found herself wide awake at six, so she got up and put on her running gear.

As she left through the back door, she noticed someone had left the gate open, and there were footprints on the path leading back to the shed. She went over to check it. It was closed, but there were scuff marks around the dirt at the base where it had been pulled open recently and a large scratch down the door. The last time she'd used it was to put the outdoor furniture away and that had been on Wednesday. It hadn't been like that then, she didn't think. She tried to figure out if anything was missing. It all looked fine though, so she closed it back up, thinking maybe she should put a padlock on it, and took off for a run down the hill and along the waterfront.

She ran back past the front door of the bookshop an hour later and saw there was something hanging from it.

Slowing to a walk and breathing heavily, Mel went to get a better look. It was a dead rat. It had been nailed through the head and its body hung down, its tail near the door handle. Mel shuddered in revulsion, looking round the empty street as if she might catch whoever had done it.

She wanted to ring Jesse, or her dad to come and get rid of it. But she knew she was being stupid. It was only a rat. There was no need to be squeamish, she told herself. It was dead. It couldn't jump out at her.

Around the back, Mel opened the shed again. She found a hammer and some garden gloves, and fished a wine box out of the recycling and reassembled it. Back at the front door she contemplated the rat. The nail was sticking out enough that she thought she could hook it out with the end of the hammer. She put on the gloves, positioned the box underneath and picked up the tool. It occurred to her that maybe the person who'd done this had used her hammer to do it. Maybe she should report it? But she'd already handled the hammer now, and she doubted the police would be that interested. It was probably kids anyway.

She took a deep breath and gingerly held up the hammer,

trying to angle it to pull on the nail without touching the dead animal, even with the gloves. She hooked the nail and tugged up, doing a girly squeal and leaping back as the nail came loose, and the rat dropped with a splat into the box. Its beady eyes looked up at her as it lay there. Mel picked up the box, and carrying it as far away from her body as she could, took it over to the bin, lifted the lid and dumped it in. She'd have to check when the rubbish collection was that week or it was going to get ripe in there in the heat.

Going back around and through the back door she filled a bucket with hot, soapy water. After she'd scrubbed down the door, she biffed the gloves into the bin. They landed mercifully on top of the rat, blocking out his stare, and she went to have a long, hot shower.

After a night spent tossing and turning, hearing noises outside every half hour and constantly checking that the doors and windows were locked, Mel finally gave up on sleep and decided to spend the day outside. She kept getting the feeling she was being watched, and needed to get out of the place and shake off her paranoia. She double-checked the alarm when she left.

Looking over towards Claire's shop, she wondered whether she was home. The boutique was closed for a couple of weeks but Claire's car was parked in the space beside her shop. There was no sign of her otherwise, though.

She took a book and walked down to Oriental Parade where she sat and people-watched and read in the sunshine for a few hours until she stopped thinking about rats and conjuring up horror stories in her head.

Ellie rang and she debated telling her about the rat drama, but in the light of day it seemed a bit silly to worry about what was probably some idiot's idea of a joke. They talked about nothing much until Ellie had to go and do a wine tasting.

~

She and Jesse had texted a few times but he was busy. His mum had a list of jobs for him and he was repairing the deck as well as helping an uncle with a roof.

It was crazy to be missing him so much when he'd only just gone. Mel worried about how she'd cope down the line when he went on his holiday. How soon was too soon to talk about moving in together? she wondered. But Nate would never let her have a dog in the flat, and Mere and Glen probably wanted their house back to themselves at some stage, not another person moving in.

She wandered home and let herself back in. Everything was normal and she breathed a small sigh of relief. She lay down on her bed and took a nap.

~

By Tuesday, Mel was happy to open the shop and looked forward to some company. They'd decided to do reduced hours over the holiday period, opening at the later hour of ten and not doing the wine and cheese evenings. It was a quiet morning and she put the time to good use, thoroughly cleaning and tidying the shelves. She had started on the kitchen when she heard the bell. Wiping her hands on her jeans, she went to investigate.

"Melody, my dear, I hope you had a good Christmas," Albert beamed.

Mel was pleased to see him and returned the smile. "I did, thank you. How about you?"

"My sister is visiting from Nelson. She flew up with my great-niece and it's always a treat to see her. At our age, you never know when it will be the last time."

That was quite a depressing thought, but Mel guessed he and his sister were lucky to have each other after all these years.

"Is there something I can help you with today?"

Albert paused, contemplating. "I don't know whether it's my place to say, my dear, but I do feel it would be remiss of me to keep silent. When I left your Christmas soiree, I noticed that young landlord of yours lurking about outside. He was on his phone and it sounded like he owed whoever he was speaking to money. I didn't like the way he was speaking and it worried me that he may come in here and upset you. I heard him mention your name."

"Well, thank you, Albert, I'll make sure to be careful. But

please, keep your distance from him yourself, won't you?"

"Don't worry about me, I don't think he even noticed I was passing. It's probably nothing to worry about, but I would never forgive myself if something happened and I hadn't mentioned it. Men like that can be very aggressive and despite the flashy way he dresses, I can't say he seems much of a gentleman."

The rest of the day was uneventful and Mel shut early. Olive had been in and had helped Mel unpack a delivery while she told her she and Colin had gone to dinner the night before to an Italian restaurant. Mel thought they were rather well suited and told her so.

"He's very proper, isn't he?" Olive said, her eyes sparkling. A proper weirdo, Mel thought, but she nodded at Olive and smiled.

That night she made cheese on toast and went to bed to watch Netflix, feeling a bit pathetic.

~

The next day was more of the same. The odd customer. A bit of cleaning and sorting and a vague sense of time going by in slow motion.

She spoke to Marion, who told her Kevin was a godsend and fitting in like he'd been there forever. He and Geoff had decided to learn moon drumming. Fern had been over, but instead of dropping the boys off, had decided to stay too. They were all having a lovely time. Mel felt a little left out until she thought about actually being there in all the chaos, and realised she was just missing Jesse.

~

When she woke up on Thursday, she was excited to be seeing him again. The shop was almost dead, so she closed at three and went to get a spur-of-the-moment mani-pedi.

As she walked down Lambton Quay, she listened to music, the sun warming her head, and she felt a deep sense of contentment with where she was at in her life. She had the shop, and Ellie. She had lovely customers, and summer stretching out ahead of her. And she had Jesse, who thought he'd be there about five, if the traffic wasn't too crazy. She hoped not.

Chapter twenty-eight

*"You must allow me to tell you how ardently
I admire and love you."*

Pride and Prejudice, Jane Austen

Traffic was awful, and Jesse had to go to his place first, so it was well after six when he got there. Mel had cracked open a bottle of Pinot at five. At half past, she decided to surprise him when he arrived and left a note on the back door telling him to come on up. He got to the top of the stairs to find her wearing nothing but the Christmas stocking necklace and a smile.

"Now that's a great way to end the year," he grinned, stripping off his T-shirt and shorts in record time and leaping onto the bed to kiss her senseless.

~

"Can't we stay here?" They lay in bed sharing her glass to finish off the bottle of red.

"No, I've been cooped up here for days," Mel complained. "I need to go out into civilisation. Besides, I promised Ellie we'd meet her at Flamingo Joe's, and you told all the guys you'd be there too."

"But I missed you. I missed this," he grumbled. He got up and headed for the shower anyway.

There was a loud slam downstairs and Mel frowned. "Did you shut the back door when you came in?"

"Yeah, I thought I did, but maybe not. I was in a rush to get up here," he said with a smirk.

Mel watched him turn and head to the bathroom, feeling warm inside now that he was back. She lay back contentedly on the bed until she heard him yell out "I need someone to scrub my back in here, any takers?"

Mel grinned and wandered into the bathroom.

"Scrubber reporting for duty," she said.

~

They made some toasted sandwiches to eat before they went and sat on the futon talking.

"So how was it back home anyway?" Mel asked. "What else did you get up to?"

"It was good. Busy. Too many sisters for one bathroom. I

caught up with a few mates and heaps of rellies. Went four-wheel-driving with some of the crew yesterday too. Oh, and I saw Reia and Ant, with Tama."

"Really, how was that?"

"They didn't see me. They were at the park when I went for a run. He was pushing Tama on the swing and she's pregnant again too, I think." Mel looked at Jesse, trying to gauge his feelings. "Hopefully it's his," he added with a little laugh.

"Was it awful?" she asked, rubbing his thigh.

"Nah, it was actually good, I think. He seems like a good dad. They looked happy. It made me realise it's time to let it go. Let Tama go, ya know. Move on. He probably doesn't even know me now."

"Aw, man, you're such a good guy," she told him fondly.

"Does that mean I get to finish last?" he asked her, pushing her back against the couch and reaching under her top with a leery grin.

"Well, you usually do anyway," she laughed.

They were a little late arriving at the bar. Skiddy, Len and Hoppy were already there, as well as Mere and Glen. Ellie arrived as they were doing a round for the table and Skiddy shot up to get her a chair from another table.

They were joined by Mark, Griff and Jono, as well as a few of Mere's friends and co-workers and Glen's best friend Dan.

After a few rounds, they decided to have some bar snacks

before they walked further towards Oriental Bay where they were going to watch the fireworks.

Mel and Jesse sat and laughed and drank and made moony eyes at each other, which the other guys gave them shit for.

Skiddy spent the whole time alternating complimenting Ellie and asking if she needed anything. He was a lovesick fool and every time Ellie talked to him, or smiled in his direction, Mel could swear she saw little hearts light up in his eyes.

Mel told them about the rat and she and Ellie tried to decide if it was something Claire was capable of.

"I know it's sexist," Ellie said, "but it doesn't seem like a chick thing to do, does it? Even if she is dying to see us leave."

"Oh, I forgot to tell you, she and Nate have broken up, apparently," Mel said.

"Really? How did you hear that?" Ellie asked.

"Olive," Mel told her. "Who was told by Colin, who she is now dating."

"Aw, cute," Ellie said. Mel told them about her confrontation with Claire and about the conversation she'd had about Nate with Albert.

"I bet it was Nate who nailed up the rat," Jesse said vehemently. "He's such a wanker."

"I doubt he wants to get rid of us though, not when he needs our rent," Ellie said.

"Do you think he's done that much coke, to go into debt?"

Jesse wondered.

"Maybe he's got a gambling addiction," Mere suggested. Her friend Rachel told them a story about a guy she knew who lost an almost-two-million-dollar home to a gambling addiction, which somehow led on to a conversation about Peter Jackson and how much property he owned, then from there to whether women found beards sexy. Glen was very much in the 'yes' boat. Ellie brought up Jesse's moustache and they all took the piss out of him for looking like a bad Billy T James character. The rat was forgotten.

~

The waterfront was heaving with people and all the bars were packed.

At about eleven, Ellie leant over to Mel, and said over the noise of the crowd, "Hey, would you mind if I took off? My head's killing me. I might go home early."

Mel was more than a little surprised. It wasn't like Ellie to be the first to leave, especially on New Year's Eve.

"Are you okay? Do you want me to come with you?"

"No, no, I'm fine. I'll try to get an Uber."

She started to do the rounds of goodbyes with the old cheesy 'See you next year' calls, amidst protests that she should stay. Skiddy, however, volunteered to go with her.

"You probably won't get a car at this time of the night," he told her. "I'll walk you. It's on my way anyway."

Mel was surprised when Ellie agreed, and they made plans

to meet up the next afternoon for a late lunch before hugging goodbye.

~

She and Jesse held hands throughout the fireworks and Mel thought how nice it was to have someone to do that with again. She had forgotten how good it was being part of a couple. Especially when everything was going well. They spent more time looking at each other than at the fireworks display, if she was honest.

"Are we going back to yours or mine?" Mel asked Jesse, as they strolled back along Oriental Parade.

"Yours? At least we can walk to your place. We might have trouble getting an Uber if we went to mine."

He had a point. The city was crowded with people. Jesse asked Mere if she'd mind letting Scrubber out when she got home — she'd be cowering under the bed, he said — and they all hugged and said goodnight and went their separate ways. Mere and Glen were headed off for a drink with friends they'd met at the fireworks.

"You happy to head back now?" Jesse asked, and Mel leant into him as they walked.

"Yep. Had enough civilisation."

He laughed. "Me too." They were both looking forward to spending some time alone.

"The weather's been amazing for Wellington." Mel was feeling happy and maybe a bit drunk.

"It's meant to turn to crap over the next couple of days. Pity, we might be forced to spend the time inside." Jesse grinned back at her.

A fire engine passed them as they began the walk up the hill towards Mel's place.

"Oh bugger," Jesse muttered. "Probably drunken fireworks users. Bloody idiots."

"Poor Scrubber. I feel bad leaving her alone when she'll be scared," Mel said sadly.

"I can almost guarantee Mere will let her sleep in with them," Jesse said with a laugh. "Under the covers too probably."

They walked in silence for a bit until they rounded the corner onto Mel's street.

The fire engine was parked out the front of her shop and it took a few seconds for her to register. Smoke poured from the upstairs window of her flat and at that moment there was a smashing sound as the glass from the downstairs window of the shop blew in.

"Oh my God." She started to run towards the shop, Jesse right behind her.

"Mel! STOP."

Mel didn't stop. In fact, she was going to run right into the shop, into the middle of the flames when an arm pulled her back.

"Mel, what the fuck?"

"George's book," she gasped. "I've got to get George's

book."

Jesse pulled her against his chest and held her so that she couldn't move.

"Are you nuts? I'm not letting the woman I love run into a burning building."

"It's the first edition," Mel sobbed. Tears rolled down her face. It wasn't just the book though, it was the months of hard work and planning to get to where they were now. All the hopes and dreams, up in flames.

"Are you the owner of the shop? Do you know if anyone was inside?" A firefighter approached her, his uniform covered in soot.

"No, no one was home. I'm the tenant. I own the shop and live upstairs. What happened? Was it fireworks?"

"We're not sure yet, we're still looking into the cause. Do you have a contact for the owner of the building?"

Mel fumbled in her bag for her phone. With her shaking hands, it took several attempts to open her contacts and locate Nate's number. The fireman noted it down and called him from his own phone. There was no reply.

"Must be out enjoying the evening. What a bugger of a thing to have to hear about. Not the best start to the New Year eh?" He looked at Mel and patted her shoulder with a beefy, gloved hand. "Not nice for you either, I imagine. I'm really sorry this has happened. Can you stay here a bit though? We're going to have to get some details. I'm Lou, I'll be back to talk to you shortly."

Mel nodded.

"I've got to call Ellie," she told Jesse. She stepped away from the noise to find a quiet spot and noticed a shadowy figure standing across the road in the doorway of the boutique. It was Claire and though she was too far away to really see her expression, her face looked stark white in the flashing lights from the fire truck.

They watched as the crew worked to bring the flames under control. Neighbours and passersby had gathered to watch too. Colin stood outside his shop, talking to Albert who was wearing a dressing gown and slippers. Someone threw a blanket to Jesse who put it around Mel's shoulders. She felt numb now from trying not to let the thoughts in her head overwhelm her. 'Nobody was hurt' was her mantra.

A police car had arrived and one of the officers was deep in discussion with Lou.

"MEL." Ellie ran towards her, Skiddy trailing behind. "Oh my God, what happened? Are you okay?"

They hugged and turned to look at the shop. Mel burst into tears again, then Ellie did too.

"I'm fine, we weren't here when it happened. They don't know how it started yet."

"Shit. But at least you're okay."

"George's book. It'll be gone," Mel wailed.

Ellie squeezed her shoulder. "Yeah, but it's just a book, Mel. There are more important things. He wouldn't care."

"I know he wouldn't, but still ..."

"I know."

"All our hard work."

"Yeah."

They looked at each other, both with tears smudging their makeup. Mel tried to wipe off a smudge of Ellie's mascara, only to make it worse. She let out a laugh. It wasn't at all funny, but at least they were in this together.

"We're insured, at least that's something," Ellie said.

Skiddy had been talking to Jesse and came over to stand beside Ellie.

"El? Are you okay?" He was looking at her with concern.

"Yeah, I'll be all right." She wiped the sleeve of her sweatshirt across her face.

He put an arm around her waist and the four of them stood, watching as huge arcs of water, rainbow hued in the light, dampened the flames.

Without any extensive knowledge of fire damage, Mel could tell by looking that everything was going to be pretty much unsalvageable. The wooden building, over one hundred years old, had gone up like a dry piece of paper.

"Hang on." Mel suddenly turned to where Ellie and Skiddy stood. "You guys turned up together, right? But you went home ages ago. And now ..."

She looked at them, Skiddy still with his arm protectively around Ellie, then turned to Jesse who was standing with his mouth comically open, staring. Mel realised that the sweatshirt Ellie was wearing was the one Skiddy had on earlier.

"No way?" Jesse said in surprise as realisation dawned on him too.

Thankfully for Ellie, if she was blushing, the flashing lights hid that fact. She cleared her throat and was about to say something when Lou came over again, and Mel introduced them.

"We haven't been able to get hold of the building owner," he told them. "We'll keep trying. I'll get some details off you in case we, or the police, need more info. I suggest you get hold of your insurance company as soon as possible too. Do you have somewhere to stay tonight?"

Mel looked at Jesse.

"You can come to my place. Of course."

"You may as well head off," he told them kindly. "We'll be here a while yet, but they won't let you back in any time soon, not with a blaze this size."

"Okay, thanks." Mel suddenly felt exhausted and slumped against Jesse.

"Come on, babe, like he said, there's no point hanging around here for now. Let's get you home."

The police had moved on to asking the bystanders if they had seen anything and the fire crew were still damping down hot spots. What a way to see in a New Year, Mel thought.

Ellie and Skiddy decided to walk back to her place and Jesse tried to call an Uber and an Ola and then finally a cab for him and Mel. New Year's Eve was the busiest night of the year and it still took some time to arrive.

It was almost four am by the time they arrived at Jesse's. They lay in bed, Mel snuggled up in the warmth of Jesse's arms but unable to sleep. Her mind was racing with the events of the night; the fire and all that would mean. Claire, Nate, then Elly and Skiddy turning up together.

Something else occurred to her then too. Something that Jesse had said when she was about to run into the burning building.

"Hey." She raised her head from where it had been resting on Jesse's chest. "Before, when you stopped me from trying to go in and get George's book, did you say you loved me?"

"Yep," he replied with a sleepy laugh.

Mel buried her head back into his chest, smiling to herself. "I love you too," she mumbled.

Chapter twenty-nine

"You may ask questions which I shall not choose to answer."

Pride and Prejudice, Jane Austen

After a fitful night full of weird dreams, Mel woke up late to find Jesse gone and Scrubber's nose lying mournfully beside her head, waiting patiently for her to wake up. She patted the covers and the dog jumped up beside her, settling down again with her head on Mel's arm as if to comfort her. Her tail wagged and she gave Mel a lick as she stroked her soft head and had a little cry.

"Well, Scrubber," she said to her new bed pal, "I hope Dad's okay with a temporary roomie."

"He is," Jesse said from the doorway. He was leaning against the frame, looking sadly at her. He was carrying a bag over one arm, coffees in a tray in one hand and a bakery bag in the other.

"I went to Kmart," he told her as he handed her the bag and set a coffee next to the bed. "Got you some stuff. And I got some Danishes." He didn't even make Scrubber get off the bed, which was a no-go zone normally, and she looked thrilled to have gotten away with it.

Inside the bag were a couple of pairs of underwear, deodorant, a plain white T-shirt, some shorts and a toothbrush. Which made Mel cry again.

"You are seriously the best," she told him.

~

Mel had only just finished showering when she got a call. It was a policewoman, asking her if she could come down to the station and give them some more information.

They drove over to pick up Ellie and Skiddy, then drove past the bookstore where tape notified the public there was no entry. A young policeman stood guard. He told her no one was allowed in yet. A few people milled around, looking official.

The building looked derelict and sad and it was awful to see.

~

They went down to the police station, checked in with the front desk and sat to wait for the officer in charge. The station was busy with people constantly coming and going. There were a lot of hungover-looking people filling out forms for lost cellphones and wallets.

Eventually, a woman in uniform came out and introduced herself as Detective Davis. She led them through to a small interrogation room and indicated to the plastic chairs.

"Please, have a seat." She sat herself and pulled out a notebook. "Look, I'm gonna get straight to the point, okay. The fire service suspects the fire was caused by arson. The investigation unit has been notified and they've sent someone out who's looking at things now."

"Arson," Mel exclaimed. "So it was intentional? Who would do that?"

"That's what we'd like to know too. We suspect an accelerant was used, but until the investigation has been done, we're merely gathering information at this stage."

"Oh my God," Ellie said.

"I'm sorry I can't tell you more, but there's a process to go through and it takes a while." She flicked through her notes and confirmed a few things with Mel from the information she'd given the fire service last night. Then confirmed where they had been, and who they were with at the time of the fire.

"We've had no luck getting hold of your landlord either. Do you have any other numbers for him, or ideas where we might find him?"

"Not really," Mel told her. "I know his parents live on the Gold Coast, maybe you can get hold of them? But I don't know their first names, sorry."

The officer wrote that down.

"In cases of arson, we always ask. Do you know of anyone who may hold a grudge against you, or the landlord, for some reason? Anything at all, it doesn't even have to be something major. We'd like to look into all possibilities, no matter how insignificant that may seem."

Mel and Ellie glanced at each other. Mel thought of the graffitied window and the rat. Perhaps Jesse's tyres being slashed had something to do with this too? But it seemed such an extreme thing to do, so evil. Surely Claire wasn't that vengeful? You never could tell someone's character from looking at them though. People were always capable of more than you thought they were.

"It's probably nothing, but my neighbour Claire who owns the boutique? Her fiancé was Nate Carmichael, the owner of the building. She's not very happy with me at the moment — I exposed him and they ended up breaking up."

Mel told her about the things that had happened and Detective Davis jotted down some details in her notebook.

"Claire was over there last night the whole time watching, though that wouldn't be normal if she'd set the fire, would it?" Mel asked. As much as she didn't like Claire, she really didn't want it to have been her.

"You'd be surprised," Detective Davis replied. "Claire McKinney?" she asked, turning back some pages on her notebook, and looked to Mel to confirm.

"Hmm, that's interesting. She was the one who called

emergency services after your alarm went off. So she was angry at you? Or at Nate?"

Mel thought for a bit. "Both, but maybe more me? I told her about a drug issue Nate has too. She wouldn't have cared about him hitting on me much, I don't think, but the drugs were a bit of a final straw."

"What sort of drugs are we talking about?" the detective asked.

So Jesse told her about his sister, and Mel relayed the conversation she'd had with Albert. They gave her Albert's details to confirm the story.

"Okay, that's all very helpful." She closed the notebook and stood up. "Thank you for coming in. I'll be in touch if I have any more information, or need any more details." She shook everyone's hands, and gave Mel her card. "Call me if you think of anything else, or need anything, okay?"

"Can I ask," Jesse said, "do you know if the buildings on either side were damaged?" He explained that he was working on the art gallery.

"I'm not sure, but I can ask," she said. "I'll let you know."

They went back out to Mere's car, blinking in the sunlight. It was all very surreal. This sort of stuff didn't happen to people like them. It was like a bad TV show, Mel thought.

"Now what?" she said wearily.

"We get drunk?" Ellie suggested.

Mel burst into tears.

Chapter thirty

"Think only of the past as its remembrance
gives you pleasure."

Pride and Prejudice, Jane Austen

They went back to Ellie's flat. She lived in a gorgeous apartment on Leeds Street. Very New York loft meets industrial, with exposed brick walls, wooden floors and a lot of stainless steel. It could have been cold and impersonal, but Ellie and Geri had a penchant for floaty, soft furnishings and rugs so thick your feet sunk into them up to your ankles. The building used to be a shoe factory in a past life and it wasn't the quietest spot at night, with a bar right across the laneway, but was great fun for people-watching.

They sat on her small balcony and drank beer.

"All that wine," Ellie said sadly. She looked at Mel. "And all the books."

"I think we can't think about it," Mel decided. "It's too fucking depressing. But even if we've lost everything, we still did it. We made a dream happen and it was so great."

"And you can rebuild, or start somewhere else." Skiddy handed Ellie a tissue.

"Maybe, I dunno," Ellie said slowly, looking at Mel.

"I can't even think of what's next," Mel said. "I want to think how proud George would have been of us, and be thankful no one was inside."

"Cheers to that," Jesse said, and they all clinked their beers. Mel looked down at her strappy sandals. They were covered in sooty marks.

"Bloody hell, I'm going to have to do so much shopping," she said gloomily. "I need running shoes, yoga gear. Bloody everything. I hate shopping."

"I seriously love you," Jesse joked, and she punched his arm, grinning.

"Want to do some stuff online?" Ellie asked "I can get you my laptop."

"Oh *man*. I need a new laptop too," Mel wailed. "And a phone charger."

She spent an hour buying some necessities and arranging delivery to Jesse's and another half hour talking to her parents and Fern, before she and Jesse headed home for an early night.

"One good thing about all this," Jesse declared, "is that you don't have pyjamas, so you'll have to sleep naked again."

The next morning Jesse got a phone call from Detective Davis. He put it on speaker so Mel could hear too.

"I wanted to let you know, the fire department has informed me that the art gallery has only minor water damage as far as they can tell. The assessor will be in touch with you as soon as possible with more details and to let you know when you can get in there. They're hopeful for tomorrow."

"Okay, that's great. Thanks so much."

"Also, I understand there were a few art pieces already there in storage?"

"Yeah, the owner had a couple of things there in the back room that was already completed."

"I don't suppose you had any security cameras?" she asked hopefully.

"Oh shit, yeah. I did," Jesse said. "I didn't even think of that but I installed some before we shut down for Christmas to cover my arse — insurance-wise — if there were any break-ins while we were on holiday."

"Can you meet me today to go and take a look at them?" the detective asked.

"Yeah, no problem. They actually connect to my laptop, so I can access them from anywhere. I could bring it down to you if you want? I don't know how much they'll show though. Maybe the one out the back door."

They arranged a time to meet and he hung up.

It felt weird not having anything at all to do, so Mel asked Mere if she would mind if she did some baking.

"Hell, no," Mere told her. "My kitchen is your kitchen. Bake away."

She put her meagre amount of clothes in the wash, wearing a pair of Jesse's board shorts rolled over at the top and a T-shirt that was too small for him. She made chocolate fudge cake and a muesli slice that she had always made for George, while Jesse mowed the lawn. She wanted to keep busy, not think too much, so she vacuumed the lounge next and gave Scrubber a bath.

~

When they got to the station, Detective Davis introduced them to a balding man with a clipboard.

"Alan, this is Mel, the tenant. Mel, this is Alan, the inspector from the specialist fire service."

He shook her hand. "I'm sorry for your loss," he said. "It's always a shock, I know. I'm almost done with my end of things and once the building is given the all clear, they'll let you back in to see if there's anything salvageable." He gave her a sad smile. "It looks like it originated in the back but there was definitely an accelerant involved, so it's done a lot of damage. Most of the building is smoke and water damaged pretty badly, I'm afraid."

Mel thanked him and they handed over Jesse's laptop.

"If you give me half an hour, I can put the footage onto

a USB and then you can have this back," Detective Davis told him.

They left it with her, and went to do some shopping for a couple more outfits and a pair of shoes to tide Mel over until her online purchases arrived.

"Want to try on bikinis?" Jesse asked hopefully. Mel laughed.

"Sure, why not. You can come into the changing room and distract me from my problems."

"Sweet," he grinned.

They walked down the footpath holding hands. Mel gave him a nudge. "Hey, I hope you deleted your porn before you gave your laptop to the cops."

It was a bit like Christmas the next day, Mel thought, as all her parcels arrived. Then she burst into tears when she realised the bear Jesse had given her was gone.

Jesse gave her a hug. "Oh, babe, I can get you another one."

"But it's not the same," she wailed.

"You've still got the necklace," he joked.

"It broke," Mel cried even harder, and then started hysterically laughing. "Sorry." She leant into his side as she blew her nose. "I'm being ridiculous."

"You're allowed," he told her. "My kuia's house burnt down once. She said it felt a bit like a death in lots of ways."

"Yeah, it does, I guess."

Jesse gave her a cheeky smile. "At least you got a free cremation though, right?"

Mel punched his arm. "Dick."

"Too soon?" he asked with a laugh.

~

They were sitting on the deck having lunch when Detective Davis rang.

"Are you both able to hear me?" she asked. "I have some news. The footage from the security was very helpful. It clearly shows the back of the bookstore and a man entering. He went to the back shed and pulled out a petrol can that he took to the back door. We're pretty sure we know who it is.

"I can't say who, but, and I'm sorry to do this, I'm hoping you can come back and do an official identification."

Chapter thirty-one

"Till this moment, I never knew myself."

Pride and Prejudice, Jane Austen

"But are you *sure* it was him?" Marion asked again.

"It was one hundred per cent him," Mel said firmly. She and Jesse were at her parents' house in the backyard sipping elderflower tonic. Fern was there and the boys were helping Kevin feed the chickens. "No doubt about it. I recognised the suit. So did Ellie."

"He seemed so pleasant at the opening night drinks though," Marion said. Again.

"When the police went to question him, he had a wall of photos," Mel told her. "All of me. Like surveillance photos. Of random things I'd been doing. He'd been watching me for months."

"Well, at least he confessed," Geoff said. "That's good,

isn't it?" It was. The police had said as much. And they had his fingerprints on the shed door.

"But *Colin*." Marion shook her head. "He seemed so unassuming."

The security footage had shown Colin Exeter clearly on New Year's Eve going into Mel's shed and bringing out a petrol can. He told police he had put it there the week before. He'd also said he was angry at Mel for rejecting his advances and for 'slutting around with that common builder'. He'd confessed to slashing Jesse's tyres, the spray-painting and the rat as well.

"I feel so bad for thinking it was Claire," Mel told them.

"Well, I thought for sure it was Nate," Jesse said. "Turns out he'd just gone on a bender and was MIA for three days. He's still a tosser though," he added.

"So now what?" Fern asked.

"The cops said he's up for ten years in prison," Mel said. "He'd been living with his elderly aunt for years apparently and after she died he went a bit loopy. Moved into his office and was sleeping in the back room on an airbed. He didn't tell anyone she had died and kept talking about her like she was fine and dandy."

"Ooh, you don't think he murdered her, do you?" Fern sounded a little bit excited.

"Apparently not, according to the coroner," Jesse said. "Sorry," he added when he saw her disappointed face.

"Well, the man was obviously not right in the head," Geoff

declared. They all agreed. Still, who'd have thought that a nasally little weasel like Colin would turn out to be such a fruitcake. Poor Olive, she'd be gutted.

"Well, it's never the ones you'd guess, is it?" Marion said sagely.

"So true," Fern said, but she was looking at Kevin as he galloped around the lawn, one boy slung over each shoulder, giggling like crazy.

Chapter thirty-two

"This was invitation enough."

Pride and Prejudice, Jane Austen

'Local bookkeeper burns down bookstore in jealous rage' the headline read in the paper. Mel sat at the dining room table, Scrubber at her feet, and scanned the article. Thankfully they hadn't mentioned her name. Just that of the store. George would have found the whole thing hilarious. Maybe he'd have written a book about it.

Her laptop dinged with an email and Mel was surprised to find it was Olive, asking if she was free to meet for a drink that afternoon. She sent a quick reply to confirm as Ellie poked her head around the door. Mel stood and flicked the jug on.

"Hey. Coffee?"

"Sure." Ellie sat and chewed on her thumbnail.

"I've been in touch with the insurance people. There's lots of paperwork we need to fill out." Mel set a cup in front of Ellie, who reached out and grabbed Mel's hand.

"Hey, don't hate me, okay?"

Mel looked at her properly and realised she was close to tears. "Why would I hate you? What's going on?"

"I got a call last night from Steve Comptom. He's offered me my old job back and I think I'm going to take it." She didn't look up at Mel as she spoke.

"Just while we rebuild?" Mel asked with a sinking feeling.

"I know this isn't what you want to hear and I love you. I loved doing this with you but I think it's more your dream than mine."

Mel stood abruptly and dumped her undrunk coffee down the sink.

"I thought we were a team. How am I supposed to do this on my own?" She turned and glared at Ellie. "So what, you're out?"

"I don't know, I just feel like it's not right for me. It's the wine side I love, not all the books and business stuff. The accounting is not my thing. I just need some time to decide."

"Well, that's great, so while you're deciding, what am I supposed to do?"

"I'm so sorry, Mel. I've been thinking about it for a while and I can't help but feel like the fire was a sign. I know you love it, and you're so good at it, but you've been practically doing it all on your own anyway."

"Even so, it's not like I can afford to buy you out, is it?"

"You wouldn't have to pay me out straight away, maybe we could work something out. I really am sorry."

~

Mel was still upset and angry when she met Olive later that afternoon. Olive looked lovely in new jeans and a pink T-shirt. Olive gave her an awkward hug. "I can't imagine how devastated you must be feeling. I couldn't believe it when I heard."

Mel hugged her back tightly and tried not to cry. "Thanks, Olive."

I've ordered a bottle of Merlot to share," Olive said as they sat. "I hope that's okay."

"That sounds perfect to me."

Olive shyly slid a package across the table to Mel. "I know it's not the same, but I got you this."

Inside was an early edition of *Pinot and Pūhā*. When she opened the front cover, she recognised George's scrawly signature.

"Oh my God, where did you find this?"

"It's not a first edition, so I know it won't replace the one you lost, but when I told the residents at work about the fire, Harry remembered he had this."

"This might be the nicest thing anyone has ever done for me," she told Olive. "Thank you so much. I really needed this after the shitty conversation I've just had with Ellie."

The waiter arrived with the wine and as he poured, Mel told Olive about Ellie's decision not to continue in the business.

"But you'll still rebuild, won't you?" Olive asked.

Mel shrugged. "I'm not sure I can afford to on my own. I'll have to pay Ellie out her share."

"That's such a shame. It was such a wonderful place." Olive looked almost as upset as Mel. "Bloody Colin Exeter. The wanker."

Mel snorted wine up her nose. She'd never heard Olive swear before. "Sorry, the romantic weekend in Christchurch is off."

Olive laughed. "I'm planning to go anyway. To tell you the truth, I was starting to have second thoughts about him. But in my line of work, any man with his own set of teeth seems like a catch."

"You can do much better than Colin," Mel told her, and as she said it she realised she really meant it.

They spent a pleasant half hour talking about various things while they finished the wine. As they were about to leave, Olive turned suddenly towards Mel.

"You know," she said hesitantly, "if you were looking for another partner, I have some money saved up. If you wouldn't find the idea unbearable, I'd love you to consider me."

Mel was taken aback. "Really? Are you serious or is this the wine talking?"

"I'm very serious. Have a think about it and let me know if you think it would work and we could go over the details."

Mel promised she'd be in touch and asked Olive to pass on her thanks to Harry for the book.

Her anger had lifted and she felt a lot lighter as she made her way back to Jesse's.

The more she thought about it, the more perfect the solution seemed. Olive shared her love of books, she was reliable and had become somewhat of a friend. And she could do the accounting, something Mel was hopeless at. As upset as she was about Ellie, she knew she didn't love books like Mel did and she was sure she'd still help out with the wine side of things. Although she was starting to feel excited about the thought of rebuilding, it was a bit daunting thinking about the months it was going to take before they'd be able to open.

~

When Jesse arrived home from work, Mel was sitting on the back deck reading *Pinot and Pūhā*.

"I've been for a wine with Olive and I realised I couldn't get back into the house," she said as he bent to kiss her. "I've got so much to tell you."

"Hopefully good things? You sound happy. By the way, I've got something for you." It was another teddy bear. Mel grinned, standing and reaching for the soft toy while she kissed him back.

"Aw, thank you," she told him, looking down at it. Then she looked closer. On his tool belt was a key. She looked up at Jesse and raised her eyebrows questioningly.

"It's a key," he said unnecessarily. "For here. I know it's not my place and maybe not ideal, but I spoke to Mere and Glen and they're more than happy to have you stay."

Mel grinned. She and Mere got on well, and they all seemed to work well together. She gave Jesse another kiss.

"So that's a yes?"

"Yes. Absolutely yes. And the good news is, I don't have to move anything in, since I only own enough to fill a small suitcase."

"Speaking of which," Jesse said, holding on to her hand and rubbing his thumb across the back of it, "how do you feel about Vietnam? Maybe Cambodia too?"

He gave her a hopeful smile. "I could use a seasoned traveller to keep me safe."

"Now that sounds like a plan," Mel said, wrapping her arms around him.

Epilogue

"We are all fools in love."

Pride and Prejudice, Jane Austen

The boat rocked gently on Ha Long Bay, the rays from the sun dappling the water. A small punt went past loaded with woven baskets of produce. Mel put down her book and reached for the sunscreen, slathering it onto her shoulders.

Looking over at Jesse she could see he was dozing, one arm flung across his face, breathing evenly.

This was their second month of travelling, having spent the first in Thailand and Laos and planning on Cambodia next.

It had been a good test of their relationship, spending every day together, and they'd only had a few minor squabbles and one more major fight. Even that seemed silly now. Mel had accidentally booked oversized luggage on a flight from Can Tho to Da Nang and Jesse had called her an idiot. It wasn't a big deal and not like it cost them a lot extra, but she'd taken offence and complained that she was doing all the work making the bookings and next time he could do it himself if he thought she was so stupid.

Even though he'd apologised, she'd sulked for a couple of hours, but when he'd tried ordering a drink in Vietnamese later at the hotel bar, he'd been so cute she'd forgiven him on the spot.

~

Mel's phone dinged and she picked it up, peering at the screen. A text from Ellie.

Weather's crap, hope it sucks there too. Please tell me you have monsoon rains

Mel laughed, took a photo which showed the railing of the boat and the cloudless blue sky beyond, and hit send.

A reply came back straight away.

Bitch! I hate you

Are you going to be home in time for Aaron's 21st?

She laughed out loud and Jesse raised his head, cracked an eye open and looked over at her.

"What's up?"

"Ellie. She wants to know if we'll be home in time for Skiddy's twenty-first."

Jesse grinned. "Does she need some help supervising?" He stood, stretching his arms above his head. "Shall we go have a cocktail? Maybe one of those Ruby Sunsets."

Mel stood as well and took Jesse's outstretched hand, the rough warmth of it by now as familiar to her as her own.

"I might even let you have the little umbrella out of mine," he added.

"Wow, what did I do to deserve you?"

"Buy me that drink and I'll show you," he winked.

About the authors

Nikki and Kirsty are sisters who love Wellington,
wine and cheese and Pride and Prejudice.

To find out more about them, or their other books, go to
www.nikkiperryandkirstyroby.com

CPSIA information can be obtained
at www.ICGtesting.com
Printed in the USA
BVHW031757030423
661674BV00012B/197